MADAGASCAR

Antisiranana

Nosy Be

N

Km 0   100   200

Miles 0   100

Mahajanga

Isle Ste Marie

Ankazobe *x*

Alivonimamo *x*   *x* Ambatoharanana   *Tamatave

Ramanandro *x*   *x* ANTANANARIVO

Anosibe an'ala *x*

Morondava *x*   *x* Longozabe

Key:

Cathedral

Churches

X Health Clinics

Set up by the McGregors

Betaola

Tulear *x*

Fort Dauphin

A Guest in God's World

The walk of life is enriched by one's companion on the trail.
Chinese Proverb

Zapf Chancery Tertiary Level Publications

A Guide to Academic Writing by C. B. Peter (1994)

Africa in the 21st Century by Erie M. Aseka (1996)

Women in Development by Egara Kabaji (1997)

Introducing Social Science: A Guidebook by J. H. van Doorne (2000)

Elementary Statistics by J. H. van Doorne (2001)

Iteso Survival Rites on the Birth of Twins by Festus B. Omusolo (2001)

The Church in the New Millennium: Three Studies in the Acts of the Apostles by John Stott (2002)

Introduction to Philosophy in an African Perspective by Cletus N.Chukwu (2002)

Participatory Monitoring and Evaluation by Francis W. Mulwa and Simon N. Nguluu (2003)

Applied Ethics and HIV/AIDS in Africa by Cletus N. Chukwu (2003)

For God and Humanity: 100 Years of St. Paul's United Theological College Edited by Emily Onyango (2003)

Establishing and Managing School Libraries and Resource Centres by Margaret Makenzi and Raymond Ongus (2003)

Introduction to the Study of Religion by Nehemiah Nyaundi (2003)

Introduction to Critical Thinking by J. Kahiga Kiruki (In Press)

Computer Programming: Theory and Practice by Gerald Injendi (In Press)

Dying Voice (An Anthropological Novel) by Andrew K. Tanui (In Press)

A Guest in God's World
Memories of Madagascar

Patricia McGregor

Zapf Chancery
Eldoret, Kenya

First Published 2004
© Patricia McGregor
All rights reserved.

Cover Picture
Sunset in Madagascar

Cover concept and design by
C. B. Peter, Todd McGregor, and Patricia McGregor

Typesetting, layout and design by
Zapf Chancery

Copy-editing by
R. Venkatasamy, PhD

Overall publishing management by
C. B. Peter

Printed by
Kijabe Printing Press,
P. O. Box 40,
Kijabe.

Published by

Zapf Chancery Research Consultants and Publishers,
P. O. Box 4988,
Eldoret, Kenya.
Email: zapfchancerykenya@yahoo.co.uk
Mobile: 0721-222 311 or 0733-915 814

ISBN 9966-9742-4-5

To

My father, Gerry Cox,who loves books
My mother, Audrey Cox,who loves adventure
My children,Corbi and Charese, who were with me in the story
And my husband,Todd, who taught me to deny myself,
take up my cross and follow Jesus.

Acknowledgements

The people who helped this book become a reality are a thousand grains of sand upon the seashore. And so I thank:

Our support team, who kept us on the mission field by their generous donations and prayer support.

Our Malagasy friends, for their warm hospitality and loving us as their own.

Archbishop Rémi Rabenirina, Ambassador Peter Smith, and the Reverend Jane Butterfield for reviewing the pre-press copy and offering valuable suggestions.

Mr. John Downing for his labor of love in scanning all the pictures in this book.

All those whose writings have been cited in this book.

My publishers, Zapf Chancery Research Consultants and Publishers, and especially my editor, the Reverend C. B. Peter for converting a bunch of printouts into a book.

And to my family, who are a constant support.

Thank you, God, for letting me be a guest in your world!

Patsy

Preface

My life is like an open book
You are free to stop and take a look.
The author is my dearest friend.
Life without Him I cannot comprehend.

All my life, I wanted to write a book, but did not have the story to tell. Going to Madagascar gave me that story. Not all our moments during our eleven-year stay in Madagascar were easy ones. Some were very trying. But all the moments—good, bad, and ugly—became colorful threads in the tapestry of my life.

Struggling with a bout of hepatitis was part of that tapestry. For two weeks I lay in my bed, unable to get out, except to use the facilities. Two weeks after that, I was able to sit up in bed. I used this opportunity to read everything I could get my hands on. Old newsletters, alumni magazines, emails—virtually anything that came my way, as I awaited my full recovery.

I cannot really remember where I came across it, but it has stuck through my mind ever since. Hundreds of years ago, two Benedictine Saints—Kevin and Bridgette—proclaimed that we are *Guests in God's World.*

I took an index card off my nightstand (all the days seemed like nights then!), wrote the saying and kept it by my side. When I was strong enough to get out of bed and get dressed, I taped the saying on my closet door, knowing I would see it at least twice a day.

For many months the saying hung faithfully on my closet door. When we were finally moving from Madagascar, I wrote it on the top of my journal. Our return to America was marked by a long series of wanderings. As we traveled from state to state, I kept reminding myself that we are *Guests in God's World.*

It happened during one of these long trips from Vermont to Florida. We were driving in an Astro van (borrowed from our parents). Our older daughter, Corbi, was sitting in the co-pilot's seat as her father drove. Charese, the younger one, snuggled with blankets and pillows in the second seat, was listening to *Odyssey* on her headset.

I asked Corbi to hand me my journal, which was in my Malagasy basket by her legs.

Written in bold black letters, she read the front of my journal, "*A Guest in God's World?* Wow, that is a great title for a book!"

And that was it. I felt that God had spoken through the mouth of my child.

As the days went by, I got truly hooked to the idea that I am a guest—of all things, a *guest*—in God's world! It revolutionized my life to look at God as my *host*. Here in Kenya, where we have been living and working since January 2003, my newfound belief in Christ as my host got strengthened by the Kenyan liturgy of the Eucharist. In the small blue booklet, *Modern Service of Holy Communion,* the minister and people have a dialogue after the Lord's Prayer, to prepare our hearts for the Sacrament. We say as follows:

Minister: Christ is alive forever.
People: We are because he is.
Minister: We are one body.
People: We share one bread.
Minister: Draw near with faith.
People: Christ is the host and we are his guests.

And that is why I decided to call this book, A *Guest in God's World.*

This book has taken quite a long time in writing. I have written parts of it in Madagascar, parts in America and the final parts in Kenya.

I offer this book to you, dear reader, not merely as a memoir, but as my sincere testimony to the goodness of God through Christ Jesus, my Lord and Savior.

Patricia McGregor
St. Julian's Centre,
Redhill, Kenya
Easter 2004

Contents

Contents

CHAPTER ONE

Into the Unknown

When you get to the end of your rope,
Tie a knot in it and hang on.

I

Jomo Kenyatta International Airport, Nairobi,
August 1991

I stared into the barrel of the gun. The soldier, dressed in army fatigues, looked impassive as he pointed a machinegun at my chest. I suddenly realized the seriousness of what I had done.

Running through the metal detectors, I had crashed the gate, threw open the exit doors and run down the ramp. On the tarmac, I had placed myself in front of the Air Madagascar plane, its door closed and pilots ready to fly. Holding my arms straight out in front of me, legs apart, I might have looked like a *"matador"* ready for a charging bull. I shouted, *"STOP THAT PLANE."*

My daughter was with me. Perhaps the two year-old innocent child seated in the stroller was what kept airport security staff from shooting at me. Or perhaps curiosity took over their minds. What was this lady with red hair and a two year-old daughter doing in the middle of the runway?

My eyes darted around the tarmac. Accompanied by another armed soldier, an Air Madagascar flight attendant drew near.

It is too late to board this flight to Madagascar. She informed me.

My mind was in a fury. *Who does she think she is talking to?* I thought to myself. *Does not she know that I have flown all the way from the USA?*

It is not too late. Open those doors! I insisted like an angry teenager shouting to his parents after being grounded. *My husband will be here any minute! We are going to Madagascar!*

It had already been a dreadful two days.

*****

Todd and I knew when we boarded the Pan Am flight from LaGuardia that we had plenty of air miles ahead of us. Being missionaries, we planned an itinerary around our pennies and decided to take the least expensive route. The schedule called for a three-hour flight from Miami to New York, followed by a three-hour layover at JFK International airport. The two-hour layover in Frankfurt the next morning would allow the four of us to stretch and stroll in the airport corridors. (At least that is what we thought). Then we would board our third flight, taking us to Nairobi, Kenya. The really long layover was to be in Nairobi, where we were to land at 9:00 p.m. and go off to Madagascar 12 hours later, at 9:00 a.m. Finally, after the three and a half-hour flight to Antananarivo, Madagascar we would reach our final destination. The total duration of the trip would be 48 hours after departure from Miami.

Packing was an ordeal. I calculated our needs, just enough to get us through a two-day flight, but not too much that it would burden us down. With Corbi, age two and half and Charese, eleven months, our carry-on luggage was filled with diapers, bottles, baby food, rattles, and a change of clothing for each of us.

Tickets, passports, money, visas, and other valuable possessions were packed in a safe place. Our minds were flooded with emotions, tears, fears, and anxieties as we traveled into an unknown land.

No one knew what we were getting ourselves into. As the first American missionaries with the Episcopal Church to go and live in Madagascar, we were trailing our own path. After a heart-wrenching good-bye to family members, we walked through customs, boarded the plane and began the trip. My ears had not even popped from the adjustment to the altitude before Charese began to get violently ill. Less than every 10 minutes she would alternate between diarrhea and vomiting, repeating this routine until all she was left with were dry heaves.

Have you ever wondered what it is like for a mother and an 11 month-old infant to spend half an hour in the small cubicle meant for a toilet on an airplane? Trust me. You do not want to know! I sat on top of the toilet seat, cleaned the vomit in the basin and changed diapers on my lap.

During our bit of reprieve on the ground at John F. Kennedy, we strolled the halls, trying to regain strength. Two hours later we were on the plane to Frankfurt. Again, a child is sick, but this time it is Corbi. I felt as though I spent more time in the bathroom substituting diapers and changing baby clothes than in my airplane seat! Vomiting, diarrhea, dry heaves! This was becoming quite alarming.

When landing in Frankfurt, medics met us at the gate. The airlines had phoned ahead and said that there was a sick child on the plane. Perhaps she would need medical care. Wrapped up in Pan Am blankets, each child was clad with only a diaper.

Hello. I heard that your child is sick. May we assist you in finding a doctor? Said a petite blonde-headed Pan-Am flight attendant. *It is easy. A doctor can come right here.*

How helpful, we thought. Todd and I talked it over briefly and decided that he and Corbi would go with the medics while Charese and I stayed in front of the gate. The medics said that the *"hospital"* was not far and they would be back soon.

The flight was scheduled to leave in two hours. When they still had not returned an hour and one half later, I began to get worried. People were boarding the flight. There was still no sign of Todd and Corbi. The flight attendants began to get impatient.

Madame, You must board the plane NOW.

NOT WITHOUT MY HUSBAND AND DAUGHTER! I exclaimed.

Madame, they continued, *the plane is going to leave any minute. In order to board, you must take the shuttle bus to the plane. You must go now.*

They say that a person's greatest weakness can also become strength. Does this include stubbornness? As I tapped my fingers on the ticket counter, I vehemently refused. Thank God I did not have to wait long. Only seconds passed and out of my peripheral vision I saw Todd and Corbi coming with the medics. At the ticket check-in counter, the medics demanded $350 in US cash!

What? $350? We tried to argue.

Well, You are Americans. Your health insurance will take care of it.

The health clinic facilitators demanded we pay the bill. The flight attendants demanded we board the plane. Knowing it was a set up; we begrudgingly handed over $350. We were categorized as rich Americans. If only they knew that our feeble missionary salary barely qualified us for food stamps in the USA.

The wheels touched down on Kenyan soil at 10:00 p.m. Booking an airport hotel was not an option for us. It would have cost an extra $50 per person for a VISA and we rationalized that for $200.00 (plus hotel) we certainly could endure one night in the Nairobi airport.

Pan Am blankets and pillows in hand (the airlines had given them to us when Corbi and Charese got sick) we sought a place to bunk down for the night. Little ventilation allowed the smoke to stand still in the air, hovering over our heads like a morning fog. Thoroughly exhausted, Corbi and Charese slept through the night while Todd and I alternated taking 'cat-naps', guarding our carry on luggage.

At 8:00 the next morning, I was feeling desperately ill. Needing to get outside to breathe some fresh air, I asked the armed guards to open the door, but someone else always seemed to have the keys. Finally, I could not hold myself together any longer. Here in the middle of the airport lounge, coming out of both ends, I lost everything inside me, including my pride of course, which is not such a bad thing.

Diarrhea ran down my leg into my socks. Vomit was all over the front of my dress. This was even more embarrassing than when the back zipper of my evening dress split at High School Prom! Always retaining his sense of humor, my husband said,

You will do anything to get a new outfit, darling.

A bop on the head is what you deserve, I thought.

My parents taught me never to shop at an airport duty free shop, as the prices would be outrageous. But, here I was, desperate to buy an African outfit. Hastily, buying the largest size with an elastic waist, I scurried to the sales counter.

You need a shower! The cashier exclaimed.

Yes, I DO need a shower. Is there one close? (The plane was scheduled to leave in less than an hour).

The cashier summoned a nearby attendant to assist me to the lady's bathroom. Inside the small cubicle was an even smaller, mosquito-infested shower. Immediately I prayed,

Lord do not let me get malaria even before I step foot on the island of Madagascar!

Turning the faucet I realized that my only "*shower*" was going to be a small trickle of cold water. Using the hotel-size soap bar and the face towel I managed to squeeze in my carry on bag, I dried my partially wet body. The clock was ticking. Our plane was to leave in less than half an hour.

Chaotically adorning my new clothes, I ran out the door. Tickets in hand, Todd was standing at attention, ready and waiting with the two girls in their strollers.

Ready to board the plane? I questioned.

Let us go! Todd answered.

Todd handed the tickets to the flight attendant,

This is not the flight TO Madagascar; this is the flight FROM Madagascar.

She looked at her watch and continued,

I am sorry to say, the flight for Madagascar has left. The next flight will be in three days.

The thought of spending three more days in the dirty, grimy, Nairobi airport, without a VISA, sounded as bad as spending three days in a prison cell. Grabbing Corbi's stroller I questioned the flight attendant,

What gate?

Gate number 1, but it has already left!

We shall see about that, I thought to myself.

Hurried and confused, I ran, pushing Corbi's stroller, down the corridor.

Todd, I will meet you there!

In 1991, the Jomo Kenyatta International Airport was structured like an American strip mall. Gate 12, where we started, was on one side of the terminal. Gate 1, where we needed to go, was on the other, all the way down a long hallway.

It was like I gained energy from a "*Power Bar*", and I scurried with Corbi down the corridor. Gate 11, 10, 9, 8, 7 ... We were making progress. A few minutes later, we finally arrived at Gate 1. But it was totally quiet. There was not a soul in sight.

I saw the plane on the runway, boarded up and ready to fly. But nothing was going to stop me! I ran past the ticket counter, through the metal detectors, down the stairs (with a two-year old in a stroller), out the door, onto the tarmac, in front of the plane, and screamed:

STOP THAT PLANE.

The pilot must have been curious of this 31-year old redheaded woman pushing a baby in a stroller. Certainly I did not appear like a typical hijacker! Gazing down on me from the cockpit, he removed his headphones and tried to communicate through body language. Leery airport personnel, accompanied by military police pointing machine guns at my chest, came closer.

Hurry, Todd! Hurry! I do not want to miss this plane!

And then, what I believe is a miracle happened. The steps were being brought to the plane! Like a little girl finding a special gift under the Christmas tree, my heart was illuminated. Out of the corner of my eye, I saw a man driving a small transport cart. The material possessions carefully packed in the three trunks and five suitcases we had chosen to haul to Madagascar for our three-year assignment, were being presented to us like a turkey on Thanksgiving Day!

It was customary in the Nairobi airport that each person had to identify each individual piece of luggage, allowing security personnel to search for bombs. Normally, no luggage was taken to the plane unless previously identified by the individual an hour before take-off.

But driving a small luggage cart, a man called out to us,

Is this your luggage?

Was he an angel? Perhaps I will never know. But moments later, every piece of our prized possessions were hauled onto the cargo department, the main cabin doors opened, and the four McGregors boarded the plane.

The plane was not even half filled. Each one of us spread out in two seats. At 19,000 feet, I gazed out the window at cotton-ball clouds and breathed a deep sigh. *When you get to the end of your rope, tie a knot in it, and hang on.*

II
The Night Betsy Prayed

Be much in secret fellowship with God...
Let prayer be the key of the morning and the bolt at night.
Philip Henry

During my 48-hour flying-through-the-sky ordeal, do you know what was happening in the United States?

At 584 4ᵗʰ avenue in Boca Raton, a 33-year old mother was having a fitful night sleep. Tossing, and turning, she pounded her pillow. She got up to get a cold cup of water. Perhaps it was the Florida summer heat, she thought, which was waking her in the middle of the night.

She checked her children. Were they all right? Did any need her assistance? Sound asleep, her children (and husband) were peacefully snuggled in their bed, dreaming away. No, it was not they. It was more.

At this moment, my sister Betsy and I were worlds apart. I was hearing the jet engine fly over Mt. Kilimanjaro in the mid-day equatorial sun. Staring out of the window, she could hear a pin drop as she spied the big dipper illuminating in the charcoal sky.

Only a few days before she and I, along with our mom and all our children, had taken our last swim together in the Atlantic Ocean. Now I was flying over Zanzibar, the well known spice island in the Indian Ocean. But halfway around the world, our spirits were still together.

She felt the Spirits urge. It was a quiet nudge that first woke her from her sleep. She was obedient. Taking the pillow from the bed, she placed it on the floor and knelt. Then she silently began to pray. For what? At that time, she was not sure. But it made a difference. It mattered to me, my family, and to the heavens.

My sister, Betsy, was awoken during the middle of the night to pray for our journey. When I came to know this, I wrote back to her. Looking back, it seems like a bit of an understatement. *I was so encouraged! We really needed your prayers!*

We arrived in Madagascar and (thanks be to God) going through customs was a breeze. The customs officer was interested in sampling only a few items of our luggage. He laughed when he saw the girls' stuffed animals! Oh, what one packs when they come from the land of Disney!

As we wrote in our October 1991 newsletter, we arrived partially intact, to a warm Malagasy welcome. Our faces brightened when we saw the sign surrounded by a large group of Malagasy people. It read, "**Mr. and Mrs. McGregor**." When they saw Todd for the first time, they said he looked more like MacGyver. The re-runs of the old series were one of the few shows on the local Malagasy TV. For some, that was their entire knowledge of an American.

Once we arrived in Madagascar, everything was closed. Because of a political turmoil, the banks, post office and all shops and restaurants were shut tight. It was quite dreary. The $350 the "medics" milked out of us in Frankfurt could have come in handy. It was very difficult to get cash.

Although we did not realize it at the time, on Aug 1st and 12th the American Embassy put out an "*alert*" requesting that all "*non-essential personnel*" (meaning women and children) leave Madagascar. Even though we had registered at the Embassy, it did not call us, for whatever reason. Looking back we are glad the Lord spared us that anxiety. Some American missionaries were held up in Nairobi for 2 ½ months, unable to return to Madagascar.

A few weeks into our arrival, Bishop Remi received a life-threatening phone call, causing him to leave his home in the middle of the night. The next day we were told that we might have to "*disappear*" also…just in case. Thank goodness nothing further developed, allowing us to stay in our home.

Now, twelve years later, I have dusted off the old journals and letters my parents diligently saved. Amongst these tattered papers I found two letters, both dated August 1991. The first is a portion from a letter I wrote my sister before leaving Florida.

I know you are going with me. I am not leaving you behind but God is bringing you with me in His special way. I know I can call upon God to send His intercessors and you will be there - praying for me, for Todd and for Corbi and Charese.

I am sad to be separated across the miles but I know this is only a temporary state. Someday we will hold hands for eternity while we worship at the throne of God, forever, together. Until that day may we both stand firm in the calling that He has given to us."

The first letter I wrote from Madagascar was also to my sister, describing the arduous journey and the political turmoil, once we arrived.

Those were our first couple of weeks in Madagascar. Do you understand why the Lord woke you up in the middle of the night to pray for us? Now, if a person does not believe that Satan might want to stop a person from doing God's will, you can just let them read this letter! It has been a spiritual warfare right from the start. But, God on the other hand, sends His faithful prayer warriors out to fight the battle (like you).

III

The Gold Wedding Band

Saying goodbye has never been easy. I guess that is why linguists have made up so many sayings such as *"See you later"* or *"Until we meet again."* Although we did not yet know it, the Malagasy have a similar sayings as well, *"Mandra-pihaona"*, pronounced *"Mahn-drah-pee-ha-onah"*. The good-byes we were to have in America meant that we would soon say hello to a new life and culture.

But now was the time for goodbyes. Goodbye to family.... goodbye to friends...goodbye from securities and the comforts of first-world living. Goodbye to a flush-toilet!

The goodbyes began in Chicago when we said goodbye to the church friends that we cherished while in seminary. Old friends, new friends, children, adults. Goodbye to Corbi's and Charese's first school. Goodbye to Corbi's kindergarten teacher whose friendship I grew to love and appreciate. Goodbye to the school moms I met every morning walking our little one's to the playground. Goodbye to the house ... to the swings, sand box and steel horsy in the park.

Helping with the transition, Todd and I felt it important to teach our children to say goodbye to all kinds of things.

After our good-byes to Chicago, we needed to say our goodbyes to Florida. To family ties and cherished friendships. Mom and Dad were happy for us, but this was not exactly what they envisioned their youngest daughter and son-in-law doing. Especially when their two granddaughters were only aged 11 and 26 months! After all, we were going into the unknown. Taking the grandkids to Africa? Who knows, they might be swallowed up by lions! (By the way, there is no Big 5 in Madagascar, just rare lemurs!)

Goodbye parties ... taking snapshots...a final swim in the Atlantic Ocean...a last minute trip to the store to buy *"just one more thing"*. The day of departure had finally arrived.

What remained of our life-long belongings (we had given away or sold 95% of what we once had). we crammed into 8 suitcases, stuffed to their full allowance of 70 pounds. Patsy was busy packing, Todd was running last minute errands, and mom was cleaning to beat the band. Perhaps it helped to keep her mind occupied rather than worrying about her daughter flying halfway across the world in just a few hours!

Patsy, give me your wedding ring and I will give it one last cleaning before you leave for Madagascar.
Good idea. Thanks, mom.

Slipping the ring off my left hand, I dropped the gold-band into hers. I went back to rolling clothes, and stuffing Band-Aids into loafers. (I realized that you could stuff more into a suitcase by rolling, rather than folding your clothes).

It was like putting a puzzle together. Each item had a place, but I had to figure out where! And there was no *"box"* to give me a visual clue! As my mind was on overload, I hardly noticed my father walking through the living room with a wrench in his hand

A few more minutes passed. Commotion was coming from the bathroom. Dad carrying a wrench? He has never been the handy man. I began to get suspicious.

Eyebrows furrowed; Mom quietly walked toward me, her lips tightly pursed together.

I have some bad news.

Bad news? What? Has our flight been cancelled?

It is the wedding ring. It has fallen down the drain. Dad and I tried to find it, but we could not. I am so sorry. A single tear snuck out of the corner of her eye, as I embraced her body next to mine.

No big deal, Mom, I assured her. *This will not affect our marriage and God is in every situation.*

I am not sure if it was the fact that I had already given up so many other things, including the car, our possessions, my dreams. What was it that caused me to react so mildly? Perhaps it was the peace of God, knowing that He was in control of all things, even the loss of a wedding ring.

Mom and I talked. I consoled her. In my process of letting go, I had given up everything. The gold wedding band seemed to be the last item to put on the altar of sacrifice. *"Resiliency is an important factor in living. The winds of life may bend us, but if we have resilience of spirit, they cannot break us."* This was good to remember, especially with the long flight ahead.

IV
Preparations

"Attempt great things for God. Expect great things from God."
The quote from William Carey was on our first prayer card. Todd and I have lived by the spirit of these great words. Without a doubt, Todd and I wanted to experience the fullness of God working in our lives. God's requirements are met by God's enabling. He will always give us the strength to do what He has called us to do. Many times the difficulty comes in discerning the call of God.

Ever so subtly, God spoke to our hearts. During an adult Sunday school class at St. David's Episcopal Church in Glenview, we began to discern the call of God. Todd and I were co-teaching a class on missions when someone asked us *"What is an unreached peoples' group?"* In his humble teaching manner, Todd explained that it is a group, which had not yet heard about Christ, and did not yet have access to the Gospel. Episcopal World Mission, our first sending agency, had five countries where they were sending missionaries: The Solomon Islands, Spain, Israel, Papua New Guinea, the Congo, and wanted to start work in Vietnam and Madagascar.

Madagascar! Where in the world is that? We looked it up on the map. Surrounded by the waters of the Indian Ocean, it is the fourth largest island in the world, approximately 350 miles off the coast of Mozambique. Of these countries, Madagascar had the greatest percentage of unreached people (60%).

Ancestral worship? That was a new religious term for me! Looking it up in a theological dictionary, I read more about it. A group of people believes that their ancestors are mediators between God and man. They worship the ancestors, taking them out of their tombs on occasion, throwing a party and re-wrapping their shrouds. (Of course that was a paraphrase!)

On a more detailed note, the Malagasy regard their country as the sacred land of their ancestors, who remain its rightful owners. The earliest Malagasy believed in a Supreme Being as well as secondary deities or spirits that haunted waters, trees, and stones. They also revered creatures such as snakes, crocodiles, and lemurs, and held that humans have spirits that do not die after bodily death.

Even today, the people believe strongly in their ancestors' power to influence disasters (such as famine, drought, and cyclones), as well as happiness, prosperity, and luck. The dead are not regarded as having departed, but are believed to remain with the family and play as important a role as they did when they were alive. Thus, they must be revered, consulted, pleased, and asked to bestow good fortune on the family. A family may throw a party in honor of an ancestor. Each tribe has its own beliefs and practices, and different ways of burying their dead. An ancestor's soul can die if it is left out of the thought of its relative. At village gatherings people ask their ancestors' permission to hold the meeting. Nobody is thought to be "dead and gone".

Reverence for one's ancestors means that one must give them an impressive farewell ceremony and a suitable dwelling place. Death is not normally a time for mourning. Without the blessing of the ancestors, nothing can go well. The Malagasy have a saying, "*A house is for a lifetime, a tomb is for eternity.*" In any case, the word "*dead*" is not used; instead, the deceased has been "*loosened*" or "*untied.*"

Few customs are stranger than that of "*famandihana*" (fa-man'DEE-an). It is practiced mainly by the Merina people of the high plateau and is regarded as a duty that the living owes to the deceased. This involves opening the tomb, removing the old shroud (called a "*lamba*") washing and re-wrapping the body in a fine new silk shroud, and then reverently replacing it back in the tomb. Since the ancestors are not thought to have departed and their spirits are very much alive, they must be welcomed, talked to, and entertained. What is important is to know that they have not been forgotten, and family members may even hum or dance for them. Tears will not please the deceased. Author Jay Heale has noted that:

> The *famandihana* can last for a day or two, which means that the family will have to hire a band, employ an *ombiasy* (witchdoctor), sacrifice cattle, and pay for food and refreshments. Even devout Christians may take part. Depending on the family's wealth, the ceremony is held every three, five, or seven years, but only during the winter months.
>
> (Jay Heale, *Culturesof the World*, pp. 81, 82)

Later that evening, after the Sunday School classes, Todd and I began to question ourselves. What is preventing us from going to Madagascar? The Bishop of Antananarivo has contacted Episcopal World Mission and requested assistance. Why don't we go there and preach the gospel?

V
Obedience to God Costs other People, Sometimes

It was a heart-wrenching departure for our family. I know it was especially difficult for my mother to see her daughter and son-in-law take her granddaughters halfway around the world. In many ways, it was probably more painful for my parents to say goodbye than it was for us. Todd and I had the confidence that we were following the will of our Lord. There was excitement in obeying the call of God on our lives.

In some ways, I was following God through Todd. I believe God had a strong call on my husband's life and if that was following him into the mission field, then I was ready to follow. I would like to give you the impression that I was whole-heartedly following my husband onto the mission field. However, that would be giving you the wrong idea. I had agreed to go with Todd to the mission field, though for him it was a bit like pulling a stubborn mule.

My dreams of a country home with a white picket fence toppled like a set of dominos. I gave into the fact that Todd and I were called to missions, but it was a painful decision.

I remembered the words of Oswald Chambers:

> If we obey God, it is going to cost other people more than it costs us, and that is where the pain begins. If we are in love with our Lord, obedience does not cost us anything; it is a delight. But to others, our obedience does cost a great deal. If we obey God, it will mean that other people's plans are upset.

Because we are so involved in the universal purposes of God, others are immediately affected by our obedience to Him.

CHAPTER TWO

First Impressions

I

A Single Stop Light

It was as if blood had been poured from a pitcher into the Mozambique channel, and swallowed by the vast ocean separating the immense island from the mainland of Africa. With a mouth as large as a ten-foot crocodile, the Betsiboka River certainly portrayed the magic of the Red Island.

It was dramatic. Coming from *"vacationland"* USA, I was used to sailboats, jet skies, motorboats, container ships, and large fishing vessels covering the turquoise ocean. In Florida, wall-to-wall high-rise buildings are-pasted like wallpaper on yellow sand.

But here, there was only solitude and desolation. Even from the wide-angle 8,000 feet view, I could hardly spot a village or a bamboo hut. All that the eye could see on this cloudless, August day was the red eroded countryside and a few fires from the slashing and burning of the forests. *Where are all the roads to this beautiful coastline?*

Finally, coastal areas rolled into hillside and then became highlands. One-room red brick houses dotted the countryside. Todd and I exchanged glances as we listened to the foreign language on the plane's intercom. We had no clue what they were saying. As we began our decent, we gave Corbi and Charese each a bottle to help

pop their ears. Stashing the travel magazine into my carry-on, I began
to gather belongings. *What is life here going to be like? What is
God going to do?*

We had finally arrived at our destination, the capital,
Antananarivo. Three green, triangular-shaped roofs accented the
black concrete walls of Ivato International Airport. With the exception
of an ancient broken down helicopter, left over from the Russian-
Malagasy partnership, no other planes were in sight.

The stairs were rolled over to allow the travelers to descend.
Disembarkment was down the stairs instead of the plane pulling up
to a moving walkway. *"Veloma Tompoko"* (ve-LOOM), said the flight
attendant. I assumed that meant *"Goodbye"*. Exhausted from the
journey, Todd and I took our time, strapped our carry-on-baggage
onto our shoulders and carried our children down the aisle, the last
to leave.

We had not realized that the airport tarmac would be our last
chance to push Corbi and Charese in strollers. As we would later
discover, it is nearly impossible to use an umbrella stroller on the
rocky dirt paths darting throughout the city. Entering the small door
leading to customs, we were quite relieved to see a man holding a
sign, **"McGregors"**.

For the first time in my life, I felt tall. At 5' 2", I am qualified as
"short" in the States. But on arriving in Madagascar I realized that
I was *tall* as I saw the welcome-party of the Malagasy people, wearing
broad smiles. The new missionaries had arrived! This was to be our
new family.

Elizabeth Rabenirina, Archbishop Remi's wife, was the first to
greet us. A kiss on the right cheek, and then on the left, while she
said *"Manahoana, Tompoko"*. (Mah-nah-OWNA, Tomb-KOO). All
that to say *"Hello!"*

"Fahasalamana?" (Fah-sah-lah-MAHN-ah). How are you?

"Inona no vaovao?" (EE—nan vow-vow). What is new?

"Tsy misy" (Tsee MEESSEE). Nothing. (Which is the typical answer).

Being not up for any language learning, I just smiled and nodded hello.

Thankfully, all eight pieces of our luggage arrived and were dragged to a Land Rover by newfound friends. Struggling with the heavy baggage, it finally dawned on me why it is called *"luggage!"* Being the guests of honor, they offered Todd and I the front, with Corbi and Charese seated on our laps. The four-wheel drive became like a can of sardines, as several people crammed in the back.

Terraced rice fields, variegated in shades of green and yellow, lined both sides of the road. Children with bloated bellies from malnutrition crowded our window, asking for a few Malagasy Francs (FMG). People bathed in the same river they drank from, hump-backed cattle at their side. Houses were 12' by 12' lean-two shacks inhabited by a family of squatters. Like a new movie seen for the first time, everything was different to me. Writings on the billboards, the unfamiliar landscape, and the strange language were all foreign! A new life was beginning for us. Not only were we on the road to our new home, but also we were on the road to new lives. Excitement and anticipation filled our hearts.

Sticking out like a lighthouse on a cliff stood a large building on top of the tallest hill. The driver pointed this out to be the *"Queen's Palace"*, the residence of the first rulers of Madagascar. Gasping on diesel fumes caused by a multitude of 20-year old vehicles, we drove through the city of over one million people. A single broken stoplight was on one street corner of the main road, Avenue Independence.

A palate of pastels colored the hillside, as houses were painted pink, yellow, green, blue and red. I watched people disappear between buildings to climb the labyrinth of paths, more numerous than the number of roads in the City. Up, up, up, higher and higher. We were now at about 4,300 feet. The narrow, windy road, not much wider than the Land Rover itself, circled the mountainside. Finally we stopped on the side of a small street.

Practically running to keep up with her pace, I followed Elizabeth down a narrow dirt path. I wondered how she walked effortlessly on this uneven path (where I later fell down!) with her high heels. I was about to stumble in my flats, not to mention what would have happened if I had heels! *She must be used to this*, I thought.

Before us was a red brick house, which was to become our humble abode. We had only two rooms to ourselves, sharing a common kitchen, dining room, living room and library with other people. I saw an outhouse, but was relieved when I found we had our own separate bathroom, equipped with flush-toilet and shower! However, in days to come, I would realize that hot water, or even the luxury of running water, was not a guarantee!

Corbi decided to check out these new toilet facilities and fell head over heals down the twenty steep, wooden steps. Quickly, we prayed for healing. The first ten minutes in our new home, and there was already a mishap! It seemed as though the spiritual battle was bearing down upon us.

I was experiencing change all about me. But really, it was I myself who was changing. My attitudes...my perceptions...my expectations of what life was all about was changing fast. At the airport, I learned my first lesson. Malagasy people are relational people. Being committed to saying hello and good-bye, I learned that they would take the whole afternoon to greet an incoming visitor.

Before coming to the airport, Elisabeth had arranged for tea to be served upon our arrival in our new home. Then we met Bishop Remi Rabenirina, our new boss.

Relationships are the key to life in the Malagasy culture. This was the first of many lessons to be learned in my new life in this new country. I had come to Madagascar to change the world, but now I realized it was really Madagascar, which was going to change me.

II
Culture Shock

To say that living in a developing country is easy would be a fallacy. If every written book explained only the wonderful aspects of missionary experience, we would be looking at the world through rose-tinted glasses. After all, if living overseas was not difficult, nor a series of challenges, then there would not be so many books written on the subject of how to adjust!

One of the books packed tightly in our suitcase was entitled *Survival Kit for Overseas Living* It was written especially for Americans planning to live and work abroad, whether in church or secular work. This book states that the success rate of overseas adjustment among Americans is not nearly as high as it might be. If left to luck, your changes of having a really satisfying experience living abroad would be about one in seven. Well, thank God that our chances do not have to be left to luck. After all, living overseas in Madagascar was HIS idea! Nevertheless, there were some very specific challenges that we faced as we adapted to the Malagasy culture.

What exactly is Culture Shock? The book *Survival Kit for Overseas Living* uses the term "*Culture Shock*" to describe the more pronounced reactions to the psychological disorientation most people experience when they move for an extended period of time into a culture markedly different from their own. It can cause intense discomfort, often accompanied by hyperirritability, bitterness, resentment, homesickness, and depression. For most people this is something they will have to deal with over a period of at least several months, possibly a year or more.

Don't we have to fight enough tropical diseases? I thought to myself. *Now we have to deal with this disease called* 'Culture Shock' *on top of everything else*! Sounds great, huh?

Here are a few of the culture shocks we were experiencing during those first few months in Madagascar:

… buying a chicken with the head still on, and the house guardian (a person who physically guards the house) hoping that the chick's head will be left over for him to eat!

… lying down on the couch and feeling something touch the back of your neck, brushing it off your shoulder, and finally realizing it was a BAT sleeping (in the middle of the day) between the folds of the blanket hanging over your couch.

… every couple of weeks or so, being awakened in the middle of the night by a light tapping noise. You think, "There must be something in the room!" Quickly you draw lots as to who is going to turn on the lights. Once the light is on, before your very eyes you see a mouse (or rat!) which you spend half an hour trying to terminate!

… when driving on the road nobody uses their brakes, but everyone uses their horn.

… being caught in a traffic jam…again and again! But it is not because of cars, but because of the cows or people pulling carts!

... being awakened at 5:00 a.m. to the sound of clucking chickens!

... going to the market and having ten people flock around you trying to sell you fruits and vegetables, and then being surrounded by numerous tear-eyed children begging for money who may sometimes even follow you home.

... the lack of conveniences such a hot water and a flush-toilet!

... the electricity going out during almost every thunderstorm. (Quite often during the rainy season)

... having three people living with you in addition to your own family and houseguests.

... having to fire your house-help because you found out she was lying to you and stealing from you. (saying the vegetables cost more than they actually did and hoarding extra money for herself.)

... stores and business being closed between the hours of 11:30 am. and 2:30 p.m.

... finding Rice Krispies on the Supermarket shelf at $7.00 per box.

... getting your pocket slashed at the main outdoor market in Antananarivo.

... not having a nursery at church for our two children during the two and one-half hour service in the Malagasy language.

... getting the order of the Malagasy vocabulary reversed and instead of *saying, "Voky be"* which means, *"I am very full"*, you say, *"Be voka"* which means *"I am pregnant!"*

Is not it great to know that our God is the God who knows all cultures, the God who knows all languages, and the God who knows all our needs, and carries us through these cultural adjustments. *"No*

*one will be able to stand up against you all the days of your lives...Be
strong and courageous. Do not be terrified. Do not be discouraged
for the Lord your God will be with you wherever you go."*
(Joshua 1:5 - 9)

III
Family Visits

For one who lives overseas, there must be no other enjoyment greater
than to have people come and visit you in your new home. I know it
was so for our family. Everything being so different, a visit from
family members brought excitement, some sort of security. It gave
us the opportunity to share our new experiences, making them real.
We were able to share our adventures of going to the market, learning
the language, finding new shops, and bargaining at the market. Since
we now became "translators" for my parents, it was an
encouragement to realize how much of the language we really
understood!

One of my most vivid memories with my parent's first visit is
walking down to Avenue Independence. On leaving our house up on
the hill, we had two options—walk the high road or the low road.
The high road would take us to the upper city and the low road
would take us to Avenue Independence. I guess we were somewhat
swayed by the time of the day. If the timing was right (we preferred
to go in the morning), it would allow us to walk down and stop by
the Hotel Colbert for a *Café au lait* and an almond croissant. This
was a bit of paradise for the new missionary. When I took this
adventure by myself, at times I would take my small pocket size
Bible and journal. While I basked in aromatic luxury, I would meditate
on the grace of God. *Taste and see that the Lord is good*!

After our luxurious morning snack, we would usually venture
to the bank. If Todd was with us, he would go ahead to do the banking
and allow us to wait at the Colbert, seeping in the wonderful aromas.

Depending on the day, the wait could be half an hour to over one hour. Time did not seem to be the issue. It was just a matter of getting money.

While Todd waited, I would take Mom across the street to the post office, where she would buy souvenirs for her stamp-collecting friends back in the USA. Of course getting across the street was no easy task. Dodging cars was difficult enough, but even more difficult was the evasion of sellers and beggars. Like ants at a picnic, men, women, boys and girls would crowd the white faced "*vahazah*," selling blue and white toy cars constructed of recycled Nestlé sweetened milk tin cans. Plastic flowers in small wooden vases were stuffed in the sellers' pockets. Spices (coffee, vanilla, and cloves) piled in grass baskets and hand-made bamboo pictures lined the pavement. If I actually wanted to buy something, I was prepared with pre-folded Malagasy Franc bills safely tucked away in my brassiere.

Madagascar, together with the islands of Reunion and the Comoros, once used to supply 80% of the world's vanilla. Most of the crop was exported to the United States and used by Hagan-Daus and other ice-cream suppliers. It was also used for the making of cola drinks, in which vanilla is an essential ingredient. However, now exports have been threatened by overproduction and the creation of cheaper synthetic substitutes. Imitation vanilla is less expensive and now lines the shelves of American grocery stores. In Madagascar, to make vanilla extract I would place a few vanilla pods in a small bottle of rum and have it soak for two weeks. The outcome? The world's best vanilla.

Vanilla is grown mostly on the hot, wet, East coast, where flowers of the vanilla orchids are pollinated by hand. Nine months later, the seedpods will be six to eight inches long. The process is labor intensive - the beans are handpicked, blanched in vats of boiling water, then dried in the sun for about five months. No wonder the high price of the vanilla bean! But not in Madagascar. Women, tying babies on their backs with colorful *lamba* (pieces of cloth), carry baskets of dried vanilla beans on their heads. The price is just a few dollars a packet.

Nothing was easy in Madagascar. Even buying stamps was quite a challenge! The downtown post office would be crowded with all and sundry. *"Lining up"* is a western cultural trait and in Madagascar one just *"pushes"* ones way up to the front. In spite of the chaos, they are very civil about the whole matter. However, if you just decide to "wait" your turn, you would be there until closing.

When you finally did push yourself to the front of stamp line, you would order the stamps at one counter, then proceed to another line to pay the cashier, and then come back to the first line to pick up the stamps. This too, could be an hour-long process.

Across the street was one of the only supermarkets in town, *"Champion"*. Mom and Dad would find this a great place. As usual, they would spoil their children and grandchildren by buying just about anything we wanted or needed. This French supermarket chain, supplied foreigners with many imported and local goods. One of the best features, was the refrigerated meat counters. The open-air meat shops on the side of the road were not adequate for my tastes. Knowing that I was buying meat without flies on it was a comfort. I tried not to think of the way the meat was transported to the supermarket.

Depending on the day and our energy, we would either end our shopping spree at the grocery store and take a taxi home (it was a long walk back uphill bearing groceries!) or continue our journey and walk down the long set of stairs to Avenue Independence.

IV
Thief! Thief!

Hilary Brandt writes that part of responsible tourism is ensuring that much of the money you spend on your holiday remains in Madagascar. That was easy for Mom. She loves to shop, and taking her to the market was always an adventure.

Especially of the time we went to the *"Zoma"*, which the Malagasy claim to be the second largest open-air market in the world. Thieves were not uncommon, although not well tolerated by the Malagasy sellers. However, that did not stop some of them from trying to rob the few tourists. One thug must have thought my mom an easy target. Putting his hand into her pocket, he tried to steal money. Being street wise, my mother noticed, grabbed his hand and yelled *"Thief! Thief!"* The robber ran away, shaken by the ordeal and aware of the possibility that if caught, he could be beaten to death.

Avenue Independence is the only wide boulevard in the capital. Although no longer clustered on this broad avenue, the *"Zoma"* used to be famous for its large forest of white umbrellas. Thousands of stalls would extend into the road, selling every product imaginable (and many unimaginable). Smiling ladies tried to sell us a goose, while young men followed us around for hours, attempting to sell us watches, or a hand-carved ship. Beautiful flowers and pots lined the street. Used clothing could be found all over. Lovely embroidered items, woodcarvings, tools, mechanical parts, automobile components, and items fashioned from recycled aluminum covered the marketplace.

A friend of mine, whose jacket was stolen (along with a lot of money) out of her locked car, saw her jacket being worn by a seller in the market.

Where did you get that jacket? My friend asked.

I bought it from someone. Said the seller.

Well, it's mine! It was stolen from inside my locked car. I would like it back, please. The kind Malagasy lady agreed.

One never knows what they might find at the marketplace.

Invisible threads in the back of our heads
Threads, which are constantly woven into webs
Webs of meaning, words unsaid
Unconscious, Invisible, What is in our heads?
What is culture? Who weaves these webs?
Meanings do not jump from heads to heads.
Messages are more than mere words that are said.
Transmitted words with messages unsaid.
Invisible threads in the back of our heads.
Threads, which are constantly woven into webs.

(Written by Patsy McGregor, December 2000, based on *Meanings in Madagascar*, by Dr. Oyvind Dahl.

IV
Facts on Madagascar

Rummaging through the closet, I finally found the World Atlas under a pile of linens. In the index, I looked up Madagascar. It was not unusual for Americans to be unaware of the location of Madagascar! If anybody knew, they seemed to have gained the knowledge from playing the board game **RISK**.

Like a puzzle piece that fits easily into the coat of Mozambique, Madagascar lies approximately 350 miles off the southeast coast of

Africa, surrounded by the shark-infested waters of the Indian Ocean. As the fourth largest island in the world, The Republic of Madagascar is its official name.

Government statistics claim that 80% of children attend school, but the average literacy rate in the country may be as low as 40%. Government publications also quote an average of 38 students per teacher. Yet Joseph, a personal friend and secondary school teacher, admits he has one class of over seventy pupils, making it difficult to teach effectively. Need I mention there are no textbooks, writing paper, pencils, or even chalk!

The road system is so complex that even a compass would get confused, let alone a visitor. Even though there are 22,800 so-called *"motor roads"*, only 10% are tarred, and only 28% permanently usable. The rest are washed away annually during the rains. Even the road to Ambatoharanana is impassible by car during the rainy seasons. A number of times Todd would have to slip off his trousers and wade up to his thighs to further his journey to St. Paul's Theological College, where we were living.

Death is common. The life expectancy is only 55 for men and three-years longer for women. Half of the population was under fifteen. White-haired old ladies were seldom seen in the villages. In spite of the death rate, population increases at an average annual rate of 3.1%, one of the highest rates in the world. At this rate, the island's population is set to double every 25 years!

Scratch a Malagasy and the blood of many nations trickles out. This local saying expresses the patchwork quilt of several nationalities within Madagascar. Four fairly large non-Malagasy groups included French, Indo-Pakistani, Chinese, and Commorean.

Madagascar has been ranked by the World Bank as being among the thirteen poorest countries in the world. But this does not inhibit the family size. For the Malagasy, the more children in a family, the more they are blessed. It is quite normal to have 8 or even 10 children in a family. One priest we knew could form a congregation with just his own family members. He has sixteen!

It took us a while to get used to eating so much rice. The locals eat it for breakfast, lunch and dinner! Rice is grown by 70% of the population and occupies about half the land under cultivation. 77% of the Malagasy people live in the countryside, but only 5% of the land is actually farmed.

> Plastic, which does not rot and comes in bright colors, is replacing the soft, natural colors of wood in the towns. Life is crowded, dusty, shabby and busy. Beggars tap on car windows with plastic mugs. Phone wires hang over the streets and are draped in untidy festoons along the front of houses. Shuttered windows are protected with burglar bars, and barbed wire tops some walls. Yet those who live in the city are the lucky ones. They have access to the limited health resources, and most of their children go to school.

(Jay Heale, *Culturesof the World*, p. 60)

In spite of its differences, this was the country, which I was beginning to love. A drastic change from the world in which I grew up, I was finding myself adjusting to the new life around me.

VII
Language School...and those L-O-N-G Malagasy Words!

I recall a time when our Malagasy teacher was teaching me to pronounce the very long verb "to scream" *"midradradradra"*. (This is what I desired to do many times when I sat in Malagasy class for a long period of time!). I asked her why the word repeated the same letters so often even when it did not change the meaning.

I also suggested that perhaps the Malagasy people would like to shorten their words in order to make it easier on us suffering foreigners trying to learn and pronounce those long and difficult Malagasy words!

Madame Lalao grinned a polite Malagasy smile and let my suggestion pass by like a bus not stopping for a passenger. Her reaction to my suggestion led me to conclude that I was not the first student to make that proposal. For numerous years, she has taught the Malagasy language to a myriad of suffering foreigners from all over the world.

Learning a foreign language is one of the most difficult obstacles a missionary has to overcome. It is also not short sighted to say that it is most probably the most important obstacle to master. The rewards are great, but they come slowly and only with great effort.

As described in Delva Murphy's book, *Muddling Through Madagascar,*

The Malagasy language is a joy to listen to but a torment to pronounce. Murphy, pg. 46

It is almost as unique as its rare lemurs, chameleons, and orchids. Cultures of the world

Within its 18 different ethnic groups, the Malagasy have one common (sort of) language. Although they have their own dialects, the national Malagasy language has words in common with Indonesian languages, and it also borrows words from Arabic, English, French, and from several other African languages (like Swahili).

With the emphasis of the first British missionaries, Malagasy words relating to religion, education, or anything literary, have an

English base. In the culinary area, items of food or drink have a
French base. Cattle and domestic animals come from Swahili, spoken
in Africa.

In 1835, the Bible was printed in Malagasy. The alphabet has
21 letters, not the 26 as in the English alphabet. Those omitted are c,
q, u, w and x. C is replaced by s or k and x with ks. The letter o is
usually pronounced like oo, as *veloma* (goodbye), which is
pronounced "ve-loom."

The general rule seems to be *"swallow as many syllables as
you can and drop the last one."* Sometimes the way one says a word
changes its meaning-*tanana* (TAN-an-a) means *"hand"* but *tanana*
(written with an accent and pronounced "ta Na-na") means *"town"*.
This can make communication quite difficult as well as humorous.

One night we were sitting at dinner. Around the table were
several of our newfound Malagasy friends, mainly students from
the theological seminary. After a satisfying meal, Todd leaned back
in his chair, patted his stomach and said, *"Be voka."* The students
burst out in laughter. He thought he was saying *"I am full"* (*Voky
be*) but instead proclaimed the surprise, *"I am pregnant!"*

Names of people and places also have meanings. Antananarivo,
the capital, means *"city of the thousands"* because it is said that a
thousand warriors originally guarded it.

The island's most famous king, whose name was commonly
known as *"Andrianampoinimerina"*, was actually a shortened the
version of his full name:

"Andrianimponimerinatsimitoviaminandriampanjaka"!

Next time you have the urge to sing in the shower, try a few of these common Malagasy phrases.

Hello   *Manao ahoana* ("mano OHN")

How are you?   *Fahasalamana*? (Fah-sah-lah-MAHN-ah)

What is new?   *Inona no vaovao*? ("EE-nan vow-vow)

No news   *Tsy misy* ("Tsee MEESS")

Please/Sorry/Excuse me   *Aza fady* ("a-za FAAD")

Thank you   *Misaotra* ("mis-OW-tr")

Goodbye   *Veloma* ("ve-LOOM")

Yes   *Eny* (AY-nee)

No   *Tsia* (See ya! As Kevin, my 12 year-old nephew, came to conclude)

See you again!   *Mandra-pihaona* (mon-dra-pee-ha-ona)

Wish you well!   *Mirary Soa ho anareo* (me-ra-ri-sue-ah who-ah-nah-re-oh!)

It is even harder than it looks! For example, the *Elementary English-Malagasy Dictionary*, published in Tana in 1969 by the Lutheran Press, explained the definition of 'accommodation' as *ny zavatra ao an-trano ilain' ny vahiny na mandry izy na misakafo*. Other definitions include 'beach' - *moron-dranomasina torapasika*; 'buffet' - *fanaka fitoeran-dovia sy hanina*; 'daytime' - *ny fotoana anelanelan by fiposahan' ny masoandro sy ny filentahany*!

Many times in my struggles, I reverted to body language - raising my arm to my mouth as a gesture for thirsty or hungry, or crossing my legs and looking impatient when having to relieve myself. It was our constant reminder that the time spent learning the language was never wasted and would giving us the skills needed to proceed with our work and make authentic friendships.

VIII
Open Fairway

Interestingly, there are two golf courses in Madagascar - an 18 hole course ten miles north of the capital, and a nine hole course in Antsirabe, a town located three and a half hours South on the only tarmacked road leading in that direction of the island. Both courses are quite unique. It is not uncommon to pause for crossing cattle or waddling ducks, and when one reaches the "*green*" on the course in Antsirabe, one is to find that it is not grass, but rather cement hard sand on which the golfer is to putt!

Todd and I played a few times on the course in Antsirabe during our times of language study, a great way to get exercise and practice new Malagasy vocabulary. "*Alefa* "(go), "*firy ny kapoka?*" (how many shots?), "*aoka*" (stop!), and to practice the new numbers learned in the classroom. I had lots of practice on my double-digit numbers!

One of these times was with mom and dad. After getting a piece of pastry at the bakery, we headed to the nine-hole course. We hired our crew. One flag bearer, one ball watcher, one sand smoother, and two caddies. We stopped playing in the middle of a hole when a "*famandiana*" (turning of the bones) came marching through. After the procession, we went back to playing golf. Dad, however, no longer had his ball on the fairway. They had taken it while walking through!

In the book *Chicken Soup for the Soul,* I read a true story about a blind professional golfer. He depended on his caddy to align his body in position so that he could swing and hit the ball. His caddy would tee the ball, align the golfers body and say *"open fairway".* The blind professional golfer would swing. Obviously, he was quite good, since he made the professional circuit.

During a four-day tournament, the blind golfer's caddie fell sick and was unable to caddie for the first two days. By the third day, he was feeling better and was watching with the other fans from the stands. The professional golfer did not seem able to do anything right. All his shots were hit right, left, hardly ever straight or "down the fairway".

From the stands, the caddie noticed that the substitute caddie was giving the blind golfer the entire rundown of the course. "There is a tree about 165 yards on your left. After that, a dogleg right. Just before the green there is a sand trap on the right.

The substitute caddie thought he was giving the blind golfer pertinent details about his game. However, what was really happening was the golfer was getting his blind eye off the goal. The professional golfer did not need to know about the obstacles, but needed to be assured that there was an *"open fairway."*

Humbly, the regular caddie asked the substitute if he could offer a hand. As he was feeling better, he would now like to assist the professional golfer. The substitute (highly frustrated at this point!) willingly surrendered and watched the caddie and golfer perform their miraculous teamwork.

The caddie teed the ball, aligned the blind golfers body and said, *"open fairway."* The blind golfer whacked the ball fantastically. It landed in a beautiful position for his next shot. Getting back his usual caddie, the blind golfer improved his scores drastically.

Truths from this story can transcend from the golf course to our everyday lives. Many times we allow the obstacles to defer us from doing our best. Instead of remembering, *"open fairway"*, we worry about the tree on the left, the lake on the right, or the sand trap just before the green. Sometimes it would be beneficial to be *"blind"* to our own weaknesses so that we would not limit God in doing our best.

IX

Omby

Corbi was beginning to speak Malagasy. *Omby* (the word for cow) was her first word. Children learn languages more quickly than adults, and the McGregor family was no exception. When Corbi prayed her first prayer, it was in Malagasy.

Before Charese too could even say 'mama', she said *"omby"*. Her first word in any language, was in Malagasy. When my sister came to visit, Corbi was the translator.

Several hundred years ago, African humped-back cattle, *"omby"*, were introduced to Madagascar. Today, a head of these cattle represents a walking bank account advertising the owner's wealth and respectability. One's importance in the local society is measured in terms of cattle, especially in the South. If one manages to earn more money, one buys more cattle. Putting money in a bank is not a popular idea. Yet the cattle's significance extends beyond wealth. The well being of the herds stand for the continuing health and prosperity of the whole group of people to whom they belong. Fat humps show the cattle are in peak condition, but quantity is still considered more important than quality! Since cattle are signs of wealth, it is not surprising that there are cattle rustlers, especially in the savannah plains of the West and the dry South.

More than 80 words (we only learned one!) in the Malagasy language describe the people's beloved cattle, and all parts of their body including horns, hump, and hide. Cattle are occasionally sacrificed to please the ancestors and are only sold if someone is very ill, or perhaps sacrificed to make that person well. After a funeral, horns will be put on the grave to show how many zebus were slaughtered for the feast, and therefore how rich and important that person was.

X
Proverbs

"Do not count your chickens before they are hatched" has a Malagasy equivalent:

"*Tsy midera vady tsy herintaona*," meaning:

"Do not praise your wife before a year". Quite an insight, Huh?

"You can trap an ox by its horns and a man by his words."

"The man who refuses to buy a lid for the pot will eat badly cooked rice."

"If you are only a dung beetle, do not try to move mountains."

XI
Baobab Trees

The baobab is sometimes described as an "*upside-down tree*" because it looks as if someone has plucked it from the earth and shoved it back in with its roots in the air. In fact, it may be wrong to classify it as a tree at all, because it is a succulent that stores water in its trunk. Unlike most trees, it does not die when the bark is stripped off. The bark is used to make fibrous cloth, baskets, strings for musical instruments, and waterproof hats. The lightweight wood is used for fishing floats and canoes. The leaves are eaten like spinach, the seeds provide oil, the empty seed husks are used as utensils, and the pulp makes a refreshing drink.

There are eight species of baobab in the world; six are found only in Madagascar, and the others in Africa and Australia. They can live for several thousand years; so many of the baobabs in Madagascar were alive long before man arrived on the island. An impressive avenue of giant baobabs stands near Morondava. (Cultures, pg. 18)

XIII
Politics

"In 1975 President Ratsiraka wrote his *Boky Mena* (Red Book) in which he adapted Marxist principles to Malagasy needs. At once the Western media, which only occasionally glances at Madagascar, yelped, "Communist!" And then they turned away again, since the island's domestic politics were not circulation-boosters. Yet within days of arriving in Tana one's antennae registered that the President is not running a Soviet-type regime, or whatever else. Madagascar's politics, like its wildlife, are unique to the island and are now evolving rapidly, unpredictably and so far not as attractively as the flora and fauna." (Quoted from Muddling, pg. 40)

XVI
My Rainforest Adventure

In our April 1992 newsletter, Todd wrote the following cover story:

I sat quietly in a small bamboo hut—a church to these rainforest villagers. It was easy to meditate in this incredible environment. The orchids painted the trees with their multicolored blossoms. The music to my ears was the calling of the aye-aye lemur, native only to the rainforests of Madagascar. Their call is loud, amplified by the echoes of the mountainous terrain.

The closest village, consisting of about 50 huts, was a two-hour walk. The closest type of "civilization" was about ninety miles away - a four to five day walk for the strongest person, and totally inaccessible by car. I had come to this area with Bishop Remi, his wife Elisabeth, and a few other dedicated walkers, on Bishop Remi's annual trek through the Malagasy rainforest.

We spent the first night in Moramanga, resting up for our 71-kilometer trek into the rainforest. At 4:00 the next morning, we would begin by flashlight. Our hopes had been to ride on the tractor, but to our dismay, it was leaving two days later, thus we began our trek on foot.

Traveling from village to village, and parish to parish, we finally approached this very remote village after four days of trekking on foot. At first sight of the Bishop, they began to clap, dance and sing a song—a song dedicated to the Bishop, sung only in the rainforest. Tears welled up in my eyes as I heard the sound of the joyous welcome. The Malagasy people were overjoyed because it was the first time Bishop Remi (and perhaps a white person) had been able to visit their remote village.

I thought of the difficulty the devoted Bishop and our group had in getting there. The Bishop's feet were covered with blisters from the several days of walking. We had to sleep on hay mattresses in the rat-infested huts. We had to survive on bland meals of rice three times a day, and put up with strict measures for the conservation of water, either for drinking or bathing.

The Malagasy in the countryside eat their meals while seated on straw mats on the floor. Forks and knives are not needed. A large spoon is used to eat rice at breakfast, lunch, and dinner. Malagasy people eat more rice than anyone else in the world.

For variety, it is cooked differently each time. "Vary soa" (watery rice) at breakfast, perhaps served with a banana, and then drier rice for lunch and dinner. The side dish is called "laoka", usually leafy green vegetables, but other times beans, fried eggs, or boiled potatoes.

Meat is only eaten on an average of once a week, as it is unaffordable for most families in this poor country. To quench their thirst, the Malagasy boil water for twenty minutes in pots containing clumps of leftover rice, which stuck to the bottom and sides of the pot at the time of cooking. A very nutritious drink containing all the vitamins from the rice, "rano vola" or "rice water" is enjoyed either hot or cold. I would fill up my thermos with this drink as I trekked from village to village, as there were no water fountains on the way!

The small bamboo church in which I sat was on the outskirts of an eleven-hut village. The sixty-member congregation owned only two prayer books. The Bishop brought some new prayer books, sold at 6.000 FMG (about $3.50) each. But this village of coffee bean growers was desperately poor. They humbly asked Bishop Remi if he knew of anyone who could donate four prayer books to their congregation. At this time, an 18-year old girl, Mary Rose, stood and presented her prayer book to the congregation.

The prayer book she offered had just recently been a gift to her from her sister. A young girl who had so little herself unselfishly gave a very precious thing to someone who had even less.

The previous day I spoke to another congregation on giving. I mentioned that giving is a reflection of one's trust in and love for God. The subject of Mary Rose's gift to the congregation was a wonderful example of unselfish giving. Because Mary Rose so vividly demonstrated God's unselfish giving, it was easy for me to donate the other three prayer books to the congregation, and give another one to Mary Rose.

Despite the physical hardships, my rainforest adventure was spiritually enriching. I saw sincere devotion and dedication that Bishop Remi had for the members of the rural churches in his Diocese. The sincere love and extension of hospitality given by these very dedicated Anglicans was inspiring. These villages, so poor in terms of material possessions, were rich in happiness and love for God. Truly, I was greatly blessed by this rainforest adventure.

CHAPTER THREE

Daily Life

Tsihy be lambanana ny ambanilanitra.
(All who live under the sky are woven together like one big mat).
[Malagasy saying]

I
My Knife! My Knife!

I sat on the couch in the strange red brick house. Here I was, living with a group of individuals from another tribe in a foreign land. But, does one "*see difficulties in every opportunity, or opportunities in every difficulty?*" I made a decision to see the cup half full. After all, we ourselves had made the decision to come to Madagascar. We might as well make up our minds to like it. When life gives you lemons, make lemonade!

I must admit, I felt it was my husband's call, but I was to follow him. Just like in the story of Ruth and Naomi. I will go where you go and your God will be my God. Yes, God (and Todd), I will follow you! I was realizing my attitude had a lot to do with happiness. I was now experiencing what mission orientation calls "*total immersion.*" I re-read my missions manual:

An overseas assignment is an enviable opportunity for expanding yourself as a human being."

I felt that I was already bursting and my balloon was about to pop. So much for expanding myself.

Under the instructions of Bishop Remi, we decided to forgo language school in the French Alps and come straight to Madagascar. Humph! Spending nine months in beautiful snow covered mountains learning French sounded nice to me. But since he was to be our supervisor, Todd and I thought it wise to follow his suggestion. English was our mother tongue and with the exception of Bishop Remi and his wife, Elisabeth, nobody seemed to understand us.

I sipped the locally made Malagasy tea and gazed up at the high ceilings. The hard wood floors were similar to the ones for which my sister and brother-in-law had paid a pretty price to install into their south Florida home. In Madagascar, those floors came naturally, with no rugs to cover the beauty of the wood. My eyes were curious and like a newborn child who sees for the first time, I wanted to soak up my new environment.

Downstairs to the right was one of the theological school's library and classroom containing a large blackboard. Chalk, however, was a challenge to find! Ten-foot high bookshelves lined three-quarter of the walls from floor to ceiling. Dickens, Shakespeare, language books and theological commentaries dotted the dusty shelves. This library was a classic. Lit only by a single 45-watt bulb, I wondered how the students could read the printed page.

Across the hallway in our home was the communal sitting room. The simple room contained an off-white couch and a single matching chair. There was a wooden coffee (or should we say tea!) table, and a bamboo shelf. The potted plant in the corner provided an additional source of life to the place.

Narrow French doors opened up to an outside garden. Yes, in the middle of a city populated with over one million, we were blessed with a garden! All around us houses sat on top of each other like matches in a box, but in our yard was green grass and a lovely jacaranda tree!

Although overgrown, the garden had some potential for development. Sometimes the unknown gifts inherited from your parents surprise you. My mom loves to garden and unknowingly, as a little girl, I learned from her the basics tricks of gardening just by helping out at her side (even when I did not want to!). Now these unspoken instructions were put into practice. Pulling weeds, rearranging flowerbeds, and planting shrubs kept me busy for the next few weeks.

Corbi and Charese enjoyed the outside and many neighboring children came over to play, stroking the green grass like a piece of velvet. The playground of most Malagasy children is a dirt floor. Children in the houses above would gaze down on Corbi and Charese, sitting on a blanket under the shade of the jacaranda tree. A few minutes later these children would bang on the metal gate, asking to play with our little ones. We found that bringing up young children on the mission field certainly had its advantages to socialization.

There was no doubt in my mind that the biggest challenge of this Malagasy home was the kitchen. Dark and dreary, it was lit with a 45-watt bulb. Pea green walls closed in the 6' x 8' space. There was one old wooden table and a very small sink. Although it was cold, I found something for which to be thankful. Running water!

I looked around for the stove, only to find a small charcoal-fueled apparatus. Cooking is not my area of expertise, and it did not look like I was going to try to improve that talent while in Madagascar. The American saying "Too many cooks in the kitchen" did not seem to filter into the Malagasy culture. Since three people slept in the small, dilapidated room off the kitchen, the dark kitchen was part of their room.

Let us realize that what happens around us is largely outside our control, but that the way we choose to react to it is inside our control. My daily prayer became, *Lord, give me grace.*

On the bright side, communal living was a great way to learn the language and culture. Daily we were learning what it was like to live "*Malagasy style.*" We learned what they ate (rice, rice and more rice!) and drank (rice water!), what they did for fun (sang) and how they spent their free time (conversing, listening to the radio). Although it nearly sent us to the psychiatric hospital, there was a lot to be said about total immersion. Joseph, the guard, Duvall and Fara became our best friends.

They adopted our children as their own. We became a family. When Charese began to talk, she would ask to be excused from the dinner table. She would toddle off to the kitchen to eat rice and *laoka* (the vegetables which go on top of the rice) with the staff. "*A man is rich according to what he is, not according to what he has.*" Here in this red brick communal house, we learned lessons of life.

One morning, I went down stairs at around 6:00 and put on some water for tea. After all, boiling water was a half hour processes in itself! As I walked into the small kitchen, our guard was in the kitchen with his foot up on the stool. He was picking his toenails with *my* knife - the one I use to cut our meat!

Exasperated but not saying a word, I went back upstairs to waken my husband.

Todd, You have got to get me out of here! I am about to lose my mind!

Why, What happened now?

It was no wonder that we had our share of medical challenges. Todd had been in hospital with typhoid after only four months of living in Madagascar. With situations like this, it is a miracle nothing worse happened.

Our guard did not wear shoes and he used a "*long drop*" toilet. Now he was using our kitchen knife to pick his toenails. Need I explain more?

II

Into the Jungle

After our arrival, the Bishop let us rest a couple of days before venturing out to what he called "*the jungle*," otherwise known as St. Paul' Theological College, located in Ambatoharanana. Ambatoharanana is 17 miles north of our home and in a very remote part of the country, accessible only by an extremely treacherous and bumpy road. Therefore, the travel time was approximately 75 minutes.

Along this adventuresome route in the Isuzu, Todd, Charese, Corbi, Bishop Remi and his son, Mamy, and I crossed over a stream about 20 feet wide with a drop of about 20 feet deep on what only can be generously called a bridge.

The "*bridge*" consisted of 30 logs, each being about six inches in diameter, lying horizontally, unattached to each other. The foundation of the logs was merely a handful of vertical beams, along with a few perpendicular beams holding the horizontal logs somewhat in place.

As we were about to cross over, we each stuck our heads out of the window to see if we were really going to make it, or if we would have to get out and walk. Get out and walk is what we had to do, because the logs shifted and the Isuzu's tires got caught in between the logs of the bridge. However, getting out of the vehicle and onto safe ground was the hard part. The bridge did not have a pedestrian walk area and hardly had a spare foot of space; so, gracefully, and one by one, we slithered out of the halted vehicle. First Todd, followed by the Bishop's son and the driver, and then the Bishop. Afterwards, I, still inside the vehicle, handed Corbi (2 years old) and Charese (12 months) from person to person, and soon we were all on solid ground.

After one and half an hour of repairing the bridge and unloading our vehicle, we were finally able to resume our journey and continue to the village of Ambatoharanana. Once we arrived, we were greeted by a few students (who had not yet left on holiday), the college administrator and his wife, and the college's two full-time faculty. Classes had just finished and would resume in late October.

The college sits on 42 acres of beautiful countryside, which was donated to the diocese in the 1880's. The college's 20 buildings sit atop a small hill overlooking the rice fields in the valley below, and the breathtaking view brings glory to the Creator.

The dilapidated buildings were in much need of repair. The dispensary never opened because of lack of finances to pay a doctor $100.00 per month to come and live in the nearby village and treat villagers and college students. The large church building was once an elegant building, but was now in urgent need of repair. Especially the roof, cracked in many places.

There is also another large building consisting of a small chapel, three classrooms, office space and a library filled with extremely dusty books, which need to be shelved and properly categorized. Very few of the books are written in the Malagasy language. Classes were held in this building as well.

Fifteen students and their families live in the eleven small brick homes located on campus. Another six Anglican students lived in town due to lack of space at the college and attended a Roman Catholic seminary.

Unfortunately, living conditions were made difficult by the fact that the only time the college has adequate water supply was during the rainy season, which lasts from November to April every year. Much of the time, however, the water was contaminated and could not be used. Therefore, the theological college was in desperate need of individuals to come forth to finance the $8,000 needed to dig a well and construct a water system.

Faithful supporters pulled through and a new water system was installed just weeks before we were to come back to the USA for our first furlough.

III
Evergreen

There are evergreen men and women in the world—praise be to God—not many of them, but a few. The sun of our prosperity makes the green of their friendship no brighter, the frost of our adversity kills not the leaves of their affection.
Jerome K. Jerome

Those first three years on the mission field were very difficult ones. Living out in a small village with no running water and two toddlers was a challenge. The closest market was a three and a half mile walk. Todd was away a lot. I was in constant struggle and was on the verge of burning out.

During one of these times of drought, I decided to "*go on retreat*" in Ambatoharanana. I wanted to spend time alone with God. Having left the children with Fara, there I was on my own to fast and pray.

I did not have to go far. Just outside our doorstep was absolute solitude. I grabbed a *lamba* to sit on, my bible, my journal, and walked out of the door.

My husband and I do not always agree. It was one of those challenging times as a couple. With missionary burnout on top of marital challenge, my condition was beginning to get critical.

As I sat under the shade of the tree, I looked up and noticed a flamboyant, or African flame tree in full bloom. Feeling righteous, I prayed, "Lord, that is always the way I want to be! Fully in bloom for you! Bright. Shinning. On fire for God."

I sat in the quiet and asked God to speak. Open journal in hand, I was ready to write.

That is not Todd, I piously thought.

Look at the beautiful tree, I thought again. *I want to continually be like that tree - always in bloom for God!* I was comparing my spirituality with my husband's, thinking mine better.

God's Spirit began speaking…urging me in a still, quiet voice.

But was not that the tree you wanted to cut down a few months ago, because it did not have leaves?

I began to see the tree differently. Just a few months ago, I thought the tree dead. With not even a bud, I saw no potential blossoms. I thought the best thing for it would be to chop it down for firewood.
Next to the flamboyant or African flame tree, was an evergreen.

Boooooorrrrring! I thought.

But that is like Todd's spirituality! Green! Always Fresh! Never changing! Solid! Not seasonal - but evergreen! He's going to make it on the mission field!

I began to appreciate my husband's spirituality and even desire that myself.

IV
Chocolate Chip Cookies

In the cookies of life, good friends are the chocolate chips!

After my first year of living in Madagascar, I finally met my heart-to-heart friend that I had been praying for. Wilma was a missionary with the Assemblies of God church. She has a very caring heart - always thoughtful towards the needs of others.

One day she drove for over an hour from her house in the city, to mine in the village, just to bring me and the girls (and of course, Todd!) chocolate chip cookies. Our friendship has remained strong until this day. Those chocolate chip cookies were one of the best investments of our life!

"On the path between the homes of friends, the grass does not grow," I recalled the Norwegian Proverb

V

Face to Face

> *For now we see in a mirror, dimly,*
> *but then we will see face to face.*
> (1 Corinthians 13:12)

While we lived in the village, it was also necessary for us to go into the city. Besides being able to take a taxi to the supermarket, or make a phone call to a friend, one of the luxuries of city living was the ability to draw running hot water from the tap. On occasion, we would allow ourselves the extravagance of getting the temperature just right, pouring in bath crystals and soaking in the tub. We would take turns on who would have the "*first*" bath water, and then who would use the same water for the second soaking.

My youngest daughter, Charese, loves to soak neck-high in a sea of bubbles. Warm water surrounding her, this is her fairyland and her time to escape the worries of life. Even when she was ten she was not too old for the rubber ducky. She would take a sundry of toys in the tub with her, preparing herself for at least a one-hour soak.

One chilly July afternoon she drew the warm water and decided to enter her fantasyland. Feeling it with her wrist, she regulated it just right and partook in a lovely warm bath.

I guess she forgot her towel when I heard her screaming at the top of her lungs, *Mom! Mom*! A few moments passed and I continued to hear the soft hum of her voice. I began to tiptoe to the bathroom, deciding to sneak upon her. *Mom, Mom*! She screamed again.

Peaking through the shower curtain, I saw my 10 year-old daughter up to her neck in bubbles; head back, floating on the water. Submerging her ears in water, she was unable to hear. Eyes closed, she was unable to see. I walked closer, bent down, and came before my daughter, face to face.

Another call came, *Mom, Mom!*

Yes? I replied. As she opened her eyes, and saw my face just inches from her own, a gasp came out of her breath.

Mom, why did you scare me like that?

I chuckled, gave her the towel, and left her alone again to enjoy the warm tub. And a thought came to me. Is not that just like us and God? We come to him, with our requests, screaming at the top of our lungs. But many times we are too busy to listen. We have our ears under water and our eyes are closed.

We ask, but we do not receive, because we are blind to His face and deaf to His voice. He comes before us, desiring to commune with His children, but we are busy in our own fantasy and fail to see Him face to face.

I found this written in a hospital. It reminded me of the face-to-face encounter with Charese.

A man yelled one day and said, "*God, speak to me,*" and a thunder rolled across the sky; but he did not listen.

Again the man said, "*God, let me see you,*" and a star shined brightly; but he did not see.

And the man shouted, "*God, show me a miracle,*" and a life was born, but the man did not notice.

So he cried out in despair, *"Touch me, God,"* and God reached down and touched the man, but the man brushed the butterfly away and walked on.

The man cried, *"God, I need help!"* and a message was written on the bulletin board with good news of encouragement, but he never bothered to read it and continued crying.

Well! A blessing is not always packaged the way you expect. Do not miss out. Jesus said: *"Do not let your hearts be troubled. Trust in God. Trust also in Me."*

VI
Heavy Load

It was not uncommon to see a pile of firewood carried on a child's back, or a pail of water transported on a woman's head, or a small child being carried on a six year-old's back. These are common sights in Madagascar.

I loved to walk in Madagascar, as one was able to see the true culture of the land and its people. One day I was passing by a man pushing a very heavy cart filled with supplies. He was pushing the cart to the next village market. Walking up a slight incline, the man began to lag. I asked in Malagasy, *"Afaka mananpyanao ve"* (*May I help you*)? Surprised at a white woman offering assistance, or the fact that I spoke Malagasy, the man gave a bewildered look on his face and cocked his head.

Just in case he was hard of hearing, I repeated myself. *May I help you push this load to the top of the hill?* Not waiting for an answer, I got behind the dilapidated cart, wooden wheels barely attached to the axle, and pushed. The combination of our strength was enough to get us to the top of the hill without too much perspiring. *Misaotra, Tompoko* (*Thank you, Madame!*) said the Malagasy man.

Tsy misy fisaorana! (No thanks necessary!), I replied and off I went.

I recalled the immortal words: "*Come to me all of you who are tired of carrying your heavy loads, and I will give you rest*". (Matthew 11:28)

One Sunday, as we were traveling to church, I saw a man pushing a heavy wooden cart up a small hill with an infant on top. The infant was having a wonderful time enjoying the ride, with a smile spread across his face. The man was perspiring and breathing deeply from the heavy load.

A brief thought came to my mind when I saw the child. As a person who seems to be looking for fun, I thought it would be so much fun to ascend the hill on top of the wooden cart, get to the top and ride down. *Wheeeeee!*

But then again, I am no longer an infant. I am not on vacation anymore. It is time for me to help push, time to stand in the gap.

Two verses from the Old Testament depict the need for an intercessor to push the heavy wooden cart on behalf of others.

Isaiah 59:16 says, "*God was appalled that there was no one to intervene*".

Ezekiel 22:30 says, "*I looked for a man among them who would build up the wall and stand before me in the gap on behalf of the land before it, so I would not have to destroy it, but I found none.*"

In this world of independence and self-exhalation, we would like the fast food method to mature Christianity. But it is time for us to move on. It is time for us to get off the cart and help push.

St. Augustine's words are thought provoking.

Without God, we cannot. Without us, God will not.

Lord, help us to be willing to get off the cart and push, to help others with their heavy load, and intercede for our sisters and brothers. Spiritual growth takes effort. Just like the father perspired with the effort of pushing his son on top of the heavy load up the hill, we are to lead others to the top. Sacrificing ourselves on behalf of one another. This is what the Christian life is all about.

VII
Spiritual Perseverance - Spiritual Recovery Rate

I laced up my Nikes and adorned my long running tights. Over them was a long pair of shorts and a long T-shirt. Putting on my baseball cap and my sunglasses, I walked out the door.

It was another bright and sunny day in Madagascar; a bit cool as it was August, one of the "winter" months. The dirt roads were quite dusty at this time of the year. We were between the rainy seasons, and the cyclone season was over. I was prepared to come back dirty, dusty and full of grime. I had asked Fara, our house helper, to gather water from the spring, put it in a pan and warm it on the small electric two-burner hot plate that usually warms our food, that is, whenever the electricity is working. If not, the water would have to be warmed on the charcoal fire. Whichever the case, the process would be a long one, and it would take over half an hour to heat water. If she began now, there might be some warm water for a bucket bath when I returned from my run.

It was an odd sight to see a woman running through small villages in the Madagascar countryside. One-room red-clay huts dotted the hills, and low in the valleys would be the farmers working in their rice fields. As I jogged down the hill from the Theological College, across the wooden bridge that our car got stuck on the very first day out to Ambatoharanana, I began to cross the rice paddies.

Going downhill is always easy. And since I had just begun, the pothole-filled road crossing the rice fields in the valley was also an easy jog. But then, on the other side, there was a hill.

It was a steady incline all the way and one needed to watch ones footing each step. It seemed as though the potholes could swallow up the largest vehicle coming, not to mention a lone jogger along the path. This road was usually impassible during the rainy season, and the public "*taxi-be*" (big "*taxi's*") would stop two and a half miles before the Theological College at Ambatoharanana. The students, faculty and others (like our family) would have to walk the rest of the way when traveling by public transportation. I would bribe my three year-old, Corbi, with a piece of bubble gum if she walked the entire way without complaining. And bless her heart, she usually obeyed happily and cherished the piece of processed sugar.

Puff, puff, puff ... uphill ... steady incline. I tried to get my breathing natural, but desperately continued sucking in air at an altitude of 4,300 feet. Cramp in my side, I tripped on a loose rock. Up, up, up.

Finally, making it to the top of the hill, I was gasping for air. I had quite a few strange looks from the farmers, knee-high in the green rice field, re-planting for the next season. Energetic children joined me along the way, only to stop halfway up the hill for lack of stamina.

Breathing deeply, I began to think I was bound to get tired after running up the hill, which was at an altitude of over 4,000 feet. But of course my body was strengthening itself for the next run. After that exercise, I would be stronger. In order to calculate my physical fitness level, the importance was in the recovery period. How quickly my body would recover from such physical exertion would determine my physical level of strength.

And so it is with our spiritual lives. When we serve God, relentlessly giving ourselves to others, we are bound to get tired. In the journey of life, there are hills, valleys and potholes along the way. The important thing is not so much getting tired, but the spiritual recovery rate. After a brief rest, are you ready to go again? Are you ready to get back on your spiritual feet and go serve God again?

Even Jesus got tired. He taught His disciples to *"Go rest awhile"*. He emphasized the need for rest and peaceful nights of slumber. And then He recovered, ready to serve His Almighty Father.

What is your spiritual recovery rate? Is it time to take a rest from the journey of life? Are you tired? Weary? Breathing deeply from the stresses of life? Jesus wants us to stop, rest, recover, and gain strength to continue the journey of life.

VIII
Dispensaries
A Vision Fulfilled ... A Dream Come True

Several years ago, it was a vision of the Reverend Canon Hall Speers to transform an old dilapidated workshop into a dispensary for St. Paul's Theological College and people of the village of Ambatoharanana. However, because of health problems, he and his family left Madagascar, and only the preparatory work of opening the dispensary was finished.

Upon our arrival, the shell of the building had been partially renovated. Lack of motivation, organization and finances prohibited this vision from becoming a reality.

Shortly after our arrival we learned of the building. Todd met with SAHASOA (The Social Development Department of the Anglican Church) and sparked a new interest within the committee about the dispensary for St. Paul's College in Ambatoharanana.

It was estimated that $5,000 was needed for this project. Individuals for staff positions as doctors, administrators, nurses and a receptionist needed to be hired and trained. Dr Zoë was hired as the first Malagasy doctor from the Anglican Church.

Staff were trained for three months by the very experienced Lutheran Social Development Department. Medicine, equipment and furniture also needed to be purchased.

Todd coordinated the fund raising effort and the $5,000 was raised. Substantial supporters of this project included Drs. Robert and Celia Brown, Messiah Episcopal Church, the local British Embassy, NOEL International, and the U.S.P.G. United Society for the Propagation of the Gospel, based in London, England.

With the help of these individuals, churches, organizations, and the prayer support of many, we were able to open the dispensary on May 23, 1992.

This was quite a triumphant day, not only for the college and surrounding villages, but also for the Anglican Church since this dispensary was the only Anglican sponsored facility of its kind in Madagascar.

It was a splendid sight to see approximately 300 villagers, college students and faculty come from all over to see the cutting of the ribbon and the blessing of the building by Bishop (now Archbishop) Remi.

Songs were sung in praise and thanksgiving and tears came to Todd's eyes as he saw this vision finally become a reality. People were invited to tour the new dispensary before going to the reception to drink warm Coca Cola and eat snacks.

The dispensary is now open to serve the College and the surrounding seven villages. It was the only dispensary open with a full-time doctor within 8-10 kilometers. Therefore, the dispensary has the potential of serving a large number of people.

The cost of the services at the dispensary was nominal, just enough to cover the salaries of the staff and the cost of purchase of medicines. Doctor's consultation is 25 cents, medicine is 30% above cost (which is still below the pharmacy cost), and free malaria medicine was given to children six years of age and under.

It is our prayer that this dispensary will bring spiritual hope as well as physical healing to the people it serves.

Each morning the dispensary is opened with a time of devotion and prayer in which everybody from the village is welcome. Thanks be to God for people like you who support our ministry and make visions become realities by being PEOPLE REACHING PEOPLE.

This was Todd's first dispensary, but not the last. Since, he has opened nine health clinics throughout Madagascar. Several of these clinics have been built from scratch. Sand has been shoveled from the bottom of the river, transported in buckets on top of heads and dried in order to make cement. Cut stone has been chiseled out of mountainsides. Boulders of heavy rock are then carried down narrow paths and brought to women who spend days pounding it by hand into small pieces of gravel used to construct the building.

Most of these clinics are in the rural parts of the country, and several have no roads leading to them. They can be reached only by helicopter or on foot. Once I flew out by helicopter for the opening of one of these health clinics in the rainforest. I was walking the 3 kilometers through the mud from the helicopter landing (open field used to play soccer) to the church and health clinic. I was approaching the clinic when I saw a man wearing a clerical collar pushing his wife in a wheelbarrow. "*Avy aiza ianao?*" I asked him. (From where have you come?) With a deep gasp for breath, he told me the name of a small village consisting of a few bamboo huts, located eight miles away.

Now, when I go to see the doctor in America, I am truly thankful that I can drive my car, park in a lot just next to the building, and then take an elevator one floor up to his office!

CHAPTER FOUR

Letters to Homeland: Our First Three Years

As soon as we settled down in Madagascar, I started writing home and receiving replies as often as the irregular postal service would allow. My family religiously preserved every letter that I wrote or received. Looking back some thirteen years now, I feel that we did a good thing in preserving all that correspondence. These letters have a versatile taste. Some tell of anecdotes and stories of our unique life in Madagascar, while others contain the outpourings of my soul before my parents and other dear ones. I have included a few of these letters in this chapter

I
Mommy, Where is the Bathroom?

7 November 1991

Dear Mom and Dad,

I am writing you a postcard from inside the land Rover, which currently has only three wheels. Moments ago we felt the left side swerve and collapse - a flat tire. We do not have a spare; so ten Malagasy men have flocked like a gander of geese around our car and are trying to assist. Thankfully, we have an English-speaking student in the car translating the discussions between Todd and his "helpers", who are expecting a few spare coins. Who knows how long we will be stuck? I would rather be a duck today; rain splashes onto the windshield and into my eyes from the cracks in the window. And I need to use the bathroom urgently. Where is the McDonalds to buy a milkshake, get out of the rain and use the facilities?

We finally arrived home and received our first letter from the US today! Because of the strike, the post office only opens once or twice a week for a couple of hours!

II
Todd Plays Cat and Mouse

21 November 1991

Dear Mom and Dad,

Our home is like grand central station at rush hour! Visitors have flocked into "our" home. During our brief three and a half months here in Madagascar, we have had almost one month filled with overnight foreign houseguests, and other periodic evenings with houseguests consisting of college students and friends. There sure is not enough time to get lonely!

I know it is always fun to receive money in Christmas cards, so here I am, a big spender, sending you 1,000 Malagasy Francs! Actually, this is equivalent to about 50 cents in US currency, but just pretend that it is worth the 1,000 that it says on the bill. At least Brian and Kevin will think it is a fortune. The Malagasy people think it is a lot. After all, it is a day's wages for our gardener and caretaker Joseph (who is paid by the college), granted he is also supplied food and housing; or a day's wages for a "nanny" or a maid, cook, or housekeeper. However, the big spenders we are, we pay Nirina and Angelina 1.500 each per day, and the Bishop says they are well paid. That is the same amount a priest here would make!

I thank God for all the help we have around the house. I guess missionary life is difficult enough with the demands of ministry with MANY people requesting our time (and money), and the bouts of loneliness resulting from missing friends and family back home. Having Nirina for the children, Angelina for the house, and Joseph for the yard and garden (and answering the "gate" bell), makes the adjustment much easier. Yesterday, as I was in bed under the doctor's orders to recover from my bout of typhoid, I was brought a lovely lunch (veal, potatoes, carrots and fresh pineapple) to my room as my children played happily outside. I most probably contracted the typhoid from Todd, whom you remember was hospitalized for a week. When he became so weak and tired that he could not walk to the doctor's, I knew it was time I fetched some students to carry him! Thanks be to God that he is now fine and has recovered from the sickness. We think it was a banana that caused the infection. We have been soaking our vegetables in bleach (to kill the bugs and to keep our hair blonde) except for the bananas, because they have a skin. However, Todd realized that he had been holding the banana whilst peeling the skin, and removing it. He then ate the banana with the same bare hand that had just been holding the banana!

One thing that is quite terrifying is seeing Todd (now that he has his energy back!) trying to catch mice that run around our house at night. Being nocturnal creatures, we are awoken many times by the sound of them scurrying underneath our bed. Last night brought about one of those amusing mice episodes. Todd and I were awoken at 3:30 a.m. to this all too familiar sound. Todd, sleeping with the flashlight close by his side, grabbed it to see where the mouse was. We saw it only too briefly, as it scurries like the wind and disappears in a flash either underneath another "protection" of bamboo furniture, or behind shoes, or through a hole in the floor. Anyway, Todd dashes out the door, closing it behind him so the mouse cannot escape, and comes back with his "weapon" – a toilet bowl brush! It did not take too long to discover that the toilet bowl brush was not a powerful enough weapon. So once again he goes carefully out of the room, and this time comes back with two long brooms. Thankfully, these weapons worked, and after an hour and a half of scurrying and searching, Todd finally won the battle of "cat and mouse"! However, in the process our room looked as though a whirlwind had passed through it! Once again, we are thankful for Joan's prayers to retain a sense of humor. I have never laughed so hard in my life!

III
An American Thanksgiving in Madagascar

25 November 1991

Dear Mom and Dad,

I am feeling much better and have gained sufficient strength. Todd seems to be fully recovered. The children still show no symptoms of typhoid, so it looks like they will be safe. Thanks be to God. You can still (and must always) pray for our good health whilst we are here in Madagascar. We have taken ALL precautions, and our arms became like pin cushions because of all the injections we were administered before arriving; but still, it is so easy to get sick. Piles of trash litter the town similar to a living room on Christmas morning after opening presents. Paper is thrown everywhere. The people who pick up the trash are on strike, so disease is even more prevalent now. Walking the few meters from our house to the main road is in single file now, due to "Mt. Trashmore" which now blocks our path.

I asked Corbi and Charese what they would like to say to GG and PopPop. Corbi's answer:

It was fun to go to the store with Daddy. A shipment came in (from South Africa) and Daddy bought me Frosted Flakes, canned Ravioli and cookies."

We did celebrate Thanksgiving and splurged with chicken, mashed potatoes and canned corn. Thank God for that shipment!

IV
Avia!

14 December 1991

Dear Mom and Dad,

The house has become quite like Christmas. Corbi, Charese and I decorated on Thursday, while Todd was at Ambatoharanana teaching. It was fun, not only for me and the children, but also for Joseph, Nirina and Angelina. The prize decoration is Gran-Cox's old table decoration—the Styrofoam carousel with Santa and the reindeer, which revolves and plays music. When we put that on the table and played it for the first time, Nirina's eyes were the size of quarters and yelled "Avia" (Come!) to everybody in the house. Joseph, Angelina and Nirina became like little children, laughing with delight and shouting "indray mandeha" (once again) as we played the carousel over and over.

V
Lifeline ... Thank God!

21 December 1991

Dear Betsy, Laura, Robin, Martha, Pierette, Ann, Kathryn, Mary Lou and Kathleen,

What a pleasant surprise and blessing from the Lord that you all called last Thursday. Truly, God knows our every need and your phone call was such an encouragement. God knows that I cannot receive letters due to the postal strike so He sent a wonderful phone call instead! Prior to your call, the holiday season had been particularly difficult. I really missed people back "home," and after Todd and I had a long talk, we finally figured out what I really missed was conversation with friends. Just three hours before your phone call I was teary-eyed and telling Todd I missed America. He said, "What do you really miss?" Besides just being with friends and family, I finally pinpointed the need. "I miss TALKING!" You know how much I love to talk and be involved in everybody's conversation. Talking with people here is such a chore, because I am either talking slowly, looking up a word in a dictionary, or having them do the same! Even with the people who speak a bit of English, I still have to explain what I mean. As Mary Lou said, it is hard to "relax" while having a conversation! Before your phone call it was particularly hard to sing Christmas carols. Every time I heard one, tears were brought to my eyes, and how I struggled with this because I love to sing, as you know! But due to the encouragement of your prayers last night, Todd, Corbi, Charese and I had a lovely time singing Christmas carols around our Xmas tree! The sadness is gone and replaced with joy, resulting from the loving intercession from special friends. Your prayers are working!

Things are changing here in Madagascar, and the town seems to be getting off its feet once again. The political situation seems to be getting in order, even though the post office just works sometimes, and nightlife is only available in three or four places. When we first came, there was a 9:00 pm curfew, and people did not go out after dark. Today, Todd and I went to a restaurant at 9:00 pm, after going to an Evangelical Christmas Concert. There were some restaurants open and even though the streets were mainly dark, some places brought about that possibility! The Malagasy do not like to go out after dark and it is mainly foreigners (and unfortunately, also the prostitutes) who go out at night.

VII
Our Wonderful First Christmas

28 December 1991

Dear Mom and Dad,

Our first Christmas in Madagascar was wonderful! We really enjoyed the English lessons and carols service held on Christmas Day evening. Yesterday was a lot of fun too, especially for the children, as the Missionary Fellowship had a Christmas party for the children. There were lots of games, snacks, cake, and even a "Frosty The Snowman" video! Corbi and Charese both loved it! We have found this missionary fellowship group to be a great blessing. Not only is it a wonderful treat to speak ENGLISH, but the fellowship and mutual encouragement of missionaries adjusting to the same culture, and kids going through the same things is edifying. On Sunday evenings at 7:30 the adults have a prayer and fellowship meeting. We sing songs, have a short meditation and pray for each other. On New Year's Day we are all gathering for a "pot-luck" picnic out in the country. Yesterday it was wonderful to ask people to translate the name of some very important ingredients for me, such as yeast, cornflower, baking powder and baking soda. Not that we have an oven, but those ingredients are important, and they are not in the French Dictionary!

Life in Tana is more "westernized" than we had imagined. By westernized we mean influenced by Americans and Europeans. Actually, we have found out that it is quite appropriate for women to wear slacks or shorts, provided that they are not too tight or too short. Thus, I have worn one of my two pairs of shorts twice, and I am quite thankful they were thrown in my suitcase. At this point I do wish I had brought a pair of casual pants, but I think I can wait until September when we shall have a list of things for you all to bring, such as tennis balls ($15.00 a can) and tampons ($18.00, available sometimes!)

We now have a pet chameleon. Its eyes turn around in a complete circle! Todd feeds it dead flies and water. I do not know if it is a pet for Todd or the kids, but he loves taking care of it!

VIII
I Must Go Down to the Seas Again

19 January 1992

Dear Friends

We have returned to Ambatoharanana from a very relaxing and enjoyable vacation in Fort Dauphin, a fairly sizable town for Madagascar, on the southeast coast. The Lutheran missionaries have a prime spot on which they own small and simple (no electricity) cabins. The location is on a small peninsula and each year they have a fellowship and business retreat at this site. This year they invited us to be part of their fellowship and indeed our time together was very enjoyable. The combination of ocean and mountains (upon one of which Patsy steadily climbed, with three other adventurers, just under two hours to the top) make a very scenic environment and the coral reefs enticed Todd to do some spear fishing for the first time. To put the icing on the cake, not only did he see some very pretty tropical fish, but he also caught one barracuda and one *lamancha*, which both make great eating. Patsy and the girls enjoyed hours on the beach playing with other children and practicing their swimming skills. Some very noticeable improvement was made by the time their vacation was over!

Now it is back to the village and our days are filled with teaching. Todd continues to teach the theological students and Patsy begins her second week of teaching the women and children. A preschool has been started for children aged 3 –5 (children of the students only) and a Children's Church will now be held on Tuesday evening at 5:00 for the children of the students, the village and surrounding villages as well. Corbi and Charese love the interaction with the Malagasy children who are now becoming friends. Todd also continues to spend many hours in preparation for the opening of the second dispensary and continuing to get the newly re-opened feeding program on its feet.

IX
Unashamed, We All Swam

January 1992

Dear Mom and Dad,

We went to a lovely lake with the Bishop and his family. There was also another couple with their children. The other couple is a neighbor and he is the headmaster at the Anglican secondary school across the "path". He also is an English professor at the university so communication is not a problem. Anyway, the lake is beautiful and so quiet and peaceful, with only a few homes on it and a lovely hotel with tennis and "mini golf". It is a two-hour drive on a very good road halfway and a very bad road halfway. So, we all went for the day and had an absolutely wonderful time. We took a picnic lunch and had quite a variety of a feast, from ham and cheese sandwiches on sliced white bread (we finally found a place which sells it), to chocolate chip cookies baked from our newly bought

oven. The Bishop's family made roasted duck, Malagasy style, a
true treat for the New Year.

Of course the serving plate of duck (and chicken) was passed
around and we could have our choice of portions. Todd and I both
passed up the Malagasy delicacy - the head (including eyeballs and
beak). Of course we were being kind and saving it for the Bishop!

The amazing thing about the trip was that everybody swam!
The Malagasy people are (mostly) very afraid of the water but much
to my amazement everybody swam! The day prior to our adventure
I went to the Bishop's house to set a departure time and I reminded
them to all take their swimsuits (or extra clothes). Some said NO
WAY – they were not going swimming. Anyway, the next day was
beautiful, and we took a blow-up large raft/small boat, which we
had bought at a garage sale and packed away in Chicago, and as
soon as we found our picnic spot, we decided to swim. Actually,
Corbi decided for us because she wanted to swim so much we just
had to go. Anyway, Corbi and I were the first ones to change and the
first ones in the water and for a while I thought we were going to be
the ONLY ones. But, slowly by slowly all the people (21 in total)
went swimming and had a blast! Of course, they did not really swim,
but they waded and some with a little bit of encouragement and a
strong hold of me, tried to float!) It was all really fun and quite
comical and very different from being in America. But that is
Madagascar! Plus, the "bathing suits" the older women wore were
quite unique…"lambas" – large sheets wrapped around them!

Boy, did we all have fun. The amazing thing also, besides
everyone swimming and taking turns in the boat, was that nobody
had been to this lake in less than 15 years! This beautiful lake! A
wonderful get away! And it is only 2 hours away (a good day's trip
if you have a car), and nobody had been there in so many years!
Most of the children had never been!

We have one more thing. We had to train Corbi to use the potty—
that is, to go INSIDE! We trained her on Tuesday and all was quite
fine. However, on Wednesday all of us as a family went to
Ambatoharanana, and the only toilet facilities at Ambatoharanana
are latrines (which were not very clean!), and a toilet, which does
not flush and does not have a lid on it. So, she opted for going
outside. After all, Ambatoharanana is a rural village and none of the
other homes have toilets, so let us fit right in!

X
O Sunshine!

26 March 1992

Dear Mom and Dad, Betsy and Ken,

We are making some improvements to our house. Our toilet is
now fixed. YEA! Celia Brown gave us money to fix it. When she
stayed here it drove her as crazy as it did us! Anyway, it is fixed and
now we have added screens to the house. YEA! This is also a good
health precaution because it keeps the flies out during the day and
the mosquitoes at night (although we did not leave the windows open
before). We also bought a set of garden furniture, comprising of 4
chairs and a round table with an umbrella, for a great price from
some people moving back to Germany. I love sitting outside in the
warm sun, protected by the umbrella, and with the view overlooking
the valley below. I have decorated it with potted plants (they also
gave us all their potted plants that needed 'TLC'). Corbi and Charese
love their new sandbox that the same people gave us as well. It was
a chore to take it apart and put back together again, but worth the
effort (especially since Joseph can help us!).

Charese is a cutie…and beginning to talk. Corbi said her first
prayer…and yes, it was in the Malagasy language (I could not

understand most of it) Charese says a couple words and understands mostly everything.

Todd is playing golf to try and take a break from his studies. You would laugh at the greens, Ken. They are sand! No joke! I guess it would be hard to keep the grass green and tidy, when the only tool they have to cut the grass is a pair of scissors! (Literally!)

XI
The Easter Bunny Hops On

April 1992

Dear Cindy and John and Friends at St. David's,

Easter was a bit drab, if we want to be honest. Joseph, our guardian, was off. He had not gone to church in over a year and really wanted to be off, so we were stuck at home for the three days. Therefore, we could not go to church and I really wanted to be in an English speaking service. But, I made the best of it (this did not affect Todd or the children as much as it did me) and boiled hot water for thirty minutes and hauled it upstairs to give myself the luxury of a hot bath. Then I sang Easter songs while soaking in the bathtub. I also managed to make a decent meal and we had three young women who are all volunteer missionaries with the Norwegians. The Easter bunny came and we had an egg hunt and had carrot cake in the shape of a bunny for dessert. Our Sunday night fellowship group met which was a blessing. Thank God for this fellowship. It is like an oasis in the middle of a desert.

Tonight is a special occasion as we have been asked over to the British Ambassador's home for dinner. I am excited and I get to dress up in the one fancy dress I brought. I even bought nail polish for the occasion!

Specific prayer requests at this point would be to pray for a 'Jonathan' for me, a friend similar to the one David had. I really miss friendships, deep meaningful friendships where you can share spiritual things and personal struggles. I have always had someone and I now feel a real void in this area. Also, of course, pray that Todd and I will work as a team and grasp the language.

XII .
A Vegetarian without Choice

26 May 1992

Dear Mom and Dad,

Hopefully, we leave for Antsirabe today. Todd had a fender-bender a couple weeks ago and it has really caused a lot of problems. It is a long and confused story, and the accident was frustrating in itself because another vehicle stopped in the middle of the road to let passengers out, with no signal whatsoever. Anyway, it was probably Todd's fault, even though it does not seem fair. The other party is trying to "milk us for everything they can," because we are white and they think we have money. Anyway, it has put added pressure on us and has blocked plans for studying because we are in Tana more than necessary. So, please pray that this will all be worked out. Todd did go to the Bishop to talk to him because these people were telling us things that sounded a bit fishy. The Bishop put us in touch with a retired insurance man who has worked for 30 years with the company. So we are in good hands. It is all very slow and time consuming, which is even more frustrating when we want to be studying the language!

Yes, Todd just returned and the people with whom he had the accident were lying to us! They do not have any insurance that covers

the estimate. The insurance company would not take us to court, as they said they would.

We may become vegetarians in Antsirabe, not because of desire, but because I have yet to find a meat market that is not open-air with flies all around. I would eat eggs, pasta, cheese, and yogurt before I would bite into a piece of that meat!

XIII
A Chicken with a Difference

27 May 1992

Dear Mom and Dad,

Had a good chicken a couple nights ago. Nobody could complain that it was not fresh! Fara had gone to buy veggies and lo and behold she came back with a live chicken (she bought it for about 75 cents!) She then asked me if I wanted her to cook it for dinner for us. "You know how? I exclaimed". She said, "Yes, as long we can find someone to kill it." (She does not like to kill them – boil and pluck only). So, we found someone to kill it, and then Fara butchered, boiled, plucked and cooked a wonderful chicken dinner with roast potatoes! A bit different than chicken breasts on the grill!

XIV
On Our Toes

26 August 1992

Dear Friends at St. Andrews,

With mixed emotions we are on the home stretch of our language school with only three more weeks of teaching left. We will finish up

around the middle of September, just before my parents come. Yes!!
Truly, I am very thankful for this time to have had a greater
opportunity to study and therefore my learning has been a bit faster
than Todd's. However, he has done quite well also, and people are
so excited when we "talk". Nevertheless, I wish we had more time to
learn the language formally. However, I then remember that our
studying the language will probably not be over for the whole time
we are here. As in seminary, our learning does not stop with the
books, but continues for many years after. I am sure many of you
can relate to what I am saying.

Learning the language for me has been the difference in adapting
to the culture and culture shock. It was such a frustration not to be
able to talk to whom I wanted. Now, if I do not want to talk to
someone, i.e. someone selling tomatoes, I can still pretend that I do
not speak the language! Ha! Ha!

We are beginning to understand the Malagasy people and we
are adapting to their customs and ways of doing things. For example,
we do not get as frustrated when we have to go to the post office and
it takes an hour to get our mail. We learn that that is the way it is
done and we cannot do anything about it. It is the same thing with
this shipment that we have been waiting for three months. Knowing
the system, helps us adapt and be a bit (just a bit) more patient.

Physically, we have been healthy (and we thank God for this)
since our last bout of whatever "tropical disease" we had; whether it
was typhoid or malaria, we are unsure. Indeed, we are also adapting
to the ups and downs of physical health and we do not take it for
granted as we might have done in the States.

The political situation continues to keep us on our toes. The
referendum is supposed to be on Wednesday. Both the government
and the opposition are ready to fight if something is started; guns
have been distributed to both sides. Our family is stocked up on

staples (rice/sugar/flour) and cash just in case banks do not open, or stores run out of stock.

If the political situation allows we hope to do some travelling with my parents in the southern part of Madagascar. They arrive one month from today; probably by the time you get this letter. People say this is the heart of the country – from where the people and their customs arise. Speaking of the political situation, you may have heard some news about the attempted coup. Well, it was not really much of anything except that a group of six boys with machine guns (not that machine guns are not a big deal!) tried to take over the radio station. This was also attempted last year before we came. Anyway, the political situation was a bit tense before the Referendum, which was held yesterday. And today I am happy to say (and so is most of the rest of the nation) that all went well and to this moment about 75% of the people voted to pass the Referendum. This means that the former president (who is corrupt) will be out of office and a new government can be installed.

XV
Milk in Our Camera

September, 1992

Dear friends at St. David's,

We are busy trying to fix up our home so it is 'livable'. As you may know, after much prayer and consideration, we have decided to live out in the small village where St. Paul's is located. Yes, the house needs a lot of work, especially in Mom and Dad's eyes, but it has been fun to see progress in even just the couple of weeks that we have been working on it. We do believe that we will have a greater impact of ministry on the students if we are able to live with them instead of just traveling back and forth daily. This will also eliminate

the one and a half hour drive on that horrible road! We will still have
the two bedrooms in town and will be able to go into "civilization"
on weekends, if desired. Some things will be necessary, such as going
to the grocery store and taking a shower. These things are not
available in Ambatoharanana since there are no stores or running
water in this town. Water has to be fetched from a spring and carried
on the head 500 yards uphill.

To answer your question, yes, we do need a new camera since
someone spilled milk on our camera while we were traveling from
Ambatoharanana to Tana. It was fresh cow's milk and placed in an
old bottle without a cap, sitting on someone's lap. The camera was
on the floor underneath their feet, but seeped through it and is now
out of order. From time to time we get great pictures, but there is no
flash, and it is not as reliable as before!

As for prayer requests, please continue to pray for the students
and administration at St. Paul's. The Anglican Church in Madagascar
is Anglo-Catholic, and is mixed in with ancestral worship and
witchcraft! We just found out that one of our students went to a
witch doctor to have a "blessing" for their child! The spiritual battle
is great; please pray for wisdom and discernment as well as strength
to fight the battle. Pray that Todd and I continue to be replenished
by the Lord to do His service here. Todd is doing a great work and is
beginning to get the student's involved in evangelism. Tomorrow
through Sunday is a big evangelism conference in which the whole
school is involved. This is a great spiritual warfare. Satan is fighting
on every side. Pray that the students would start to serve God. Some
students are here because it is a "job". Since they get a monthly
bursary, they are not at the college because they are really called by
the Lord. Pray that those who are not called into the ministry be
released in some way, and those who are called would be zealous for
the Lord. Todd is planning an evangelism conference and church
planting during July/August. There is a SOMA (Sharing of Overseas
Ministry Abroad) team coming from Australia during the month of

August who will help out with the evangelism crusade. Pray for Todd's leadership and wisdom in this event. Pray for people to be thirsty for the Lord. Pray for them to see the serious danger of witchcraft and ancestral worship and pray for them to see the Lord instead.

XVI
I Don't Want School; I want the Girls

November 1992

Dear Mom and Dad.

While Todd and I played tennis on the very fast dirt courts, Corbi and Charese had a picnic by the pool with Nirina who we hired for the afternoon to come with us (for 50 cents). Nirina had never been in a swimming pool and did not have a bathing suit, so I lent her my purple leotard and it worked just fine.

Later, we found that Nirina was crying. (An explanation from her lasted a couple of hours because of barriers in translation and having to look up every other word in the dictionary)." When asked why she was crying, the answer was because she found out someone else would be taking care of Corbi and Charese when Todd and I travel to the college (Ambatoharanana). When I asked her about her schooling, she said she did not want to go to high school because she wanted to take care of Corbi and Charese. But we explained to her that education was very important and she must go to school. To complicate the story further, she revealed that she did not have enough money to buy supplies and clothing in order to go to school, and she would rather take care of Corbi and Charese for 75 cents a day! So ... what to do? Todd and I talked it over and decided that school is very important, and she must go. We told her we would give her some clothing but not until the first day of school (to make sure she actually went). So again…for the third time and for various people,

I went through my wardrobe to see what I could spare ... and gave her a dress, a skirt, a jacket, and two tops. We also put in some school supplies. Nirina was delighted! We hope and pray this will bring her some motivation to learn.

It is so hard to know to what extent to go to in order to help someone. Dealing with the poverty here in MADA is a struggle. Todd and I cannot walk down the street without a beggar or a crippled person coming to ask for money. What do we do? Do we give them some change (which we did on one occasion) and have all the other children come "out of the woodwork" and flock to us as well? Do we close our eyes and try to deny the hungry baby on the beggars back? It is a most difficult situation. Both Todd and I are in prayer about it. Of course it makes one think…is what I am doing with my money what God wants me (or us) to do? Is it being a good steward of our money to buy that electric beater to make mashed potatoes for our children, when there are people starving on the street and do not even have potatoes to eat? Is it being a good steward of our money to join that tennis club (for a very inexpensive price) when there are people who do not even have a house to live in? These are struggles we are dealing with and praying about, struggles, which they warned us of in Missionary Internship. Do we live exactly like the Malagasy people, or do we share some of the blessings that God has given us because we have come from a rich country?

All of these questions do not really have answers, except we did buy that electric beater (and the mashed potatoes were a great change from boiled or fried), and we did join that tennis club! I guess it all comes down from being a good steward of our gifts. I believe we are good stewards of our gift of children when we help make them happy, even if it be through mashed potatoes or a swim in the pool! We are careful not to be stingy or selfish with our money, and to be generous and giving because it is God who has given to us all. So, the bottom line is that we pray about where God wants us to put our money. This is a new struggle for us, but perhaps you have been in this dilemma or felt this struggle before (I know Dad did when deciding on whether or not to join the golf club when his daughter and husband were going to live in Madagascar!).

XVII
The Kid Guests

November 1992

Dear Betsy-

Last night Corbi and Charese had their first guests for the night. A missionary's daughter who just turned four had a party which Corbi and Charese attended. After the party they still wanted to play (of course!) so I invited them to come to Ambatoharanana for the night. They were overjoyed until the time they had to go to bed and then both girls (four and six) cried and cried for their mommy! Well it is not like we can just hop right into the car and take them home. Nor could we pick up the phone and request their mother to assure them it will be all right and it would not be that long until morning! Finally, after some talking and re-assuring, they requested me to leave the light on because they were afraid of the dark. The hall light was not sufficient, but it had to be the overhead light in their room. Since Corbi and Charese do not sleep with the light on, they thought it was PLAY time. So I decided to let them go and play themselves to sleep! Before I hit the sack, the room was very quiet so I peaked in to assure myself they were all fast asleep. Well, they were, all, except Corbi, who was very quietly sitting up in her sleeping bag playing with Play-doe!

XVIII
Its Nice, but the Hawk Lurks Around

4 November 1992

Letter "home"

Greetings to you all from the small village of Ambatoharanana! I am one day behind on my goal of writing you all each week. I desire to do it Wednesday but Thursday is good because then I can give this letter to Naina (the driver and student who lives in town) so that he can mail it on Friday. So, that is my goal, to write every week and have it sent each Friday. This is letter number one from Ambatoharanana.

All is well here in Ambatoharanana. Our house is looking better everyday. Mom and Dad, you would really notice a difference! Our kitchen has been painted white and with the red cherries as tablecloth and curtains it really looks nice. Our refrigerator and stove have been moved here, so it makes cooking a bit more difficult in Tana, but then again we are not there as much and there are many good places to eat!! Other improvements include putting straw matting on the banister, and the workers have stabilized it in such a way that it is now stronger; putting straw matting up in the bathroom (around the bathtub and wall) just to make it look nicer; making pillows and other items just for enhancing the beauty and comfort; and hanging up Betsy's beautiful picture that she gave me. As you can testify, Mom, it fits in with the color scheme beautifully! I love it. Our house in Ambatoharanana is really beginning to look and feel like home. Fara's room was painted as well, so this helps her to enjoy it here also.

The students, workers and other colleagues love it that we are living here. I have already noticed a great change. They really appreciate the fact that we live out here with them and can be a part of their life here, instead of always being a visitor who travels back and forth. The guys continue to play a lot of sports, which is fun to watch and participate in.

We continue to have a house filled with visitors and animals - some wanted and some not so wanted. Another visitor arrives today, Mr. Bacon from the USPG in England. He will stay out here in Ambatoharanana today and tomorrow, and go into town with us on Saturday. Rev. David Purdy has also been our dining guest out here in Ambatoharanana. For the sleeping, however, he has been able to stay at Flaurant's house since he is away for the week. Hall Speers has still not arrived back from Toamasina, perhaps because he is still discussing things with Bishop Donald Smith or perhaps because of the gas situation. Who knows? All we know is that he has not arrived yet.

As far as the animals, the hawk continues to lurk outside our bedroom door. I would assume that the eggs would have hatched by now but if so we have not heard a cheep out of the youngsters. It does not really matter now, especially when the hawk is lurking around. Charese certainly remembers her encounter with the hawk and does not want to go out on the balcony, which is good because it will not be fixed until we buy the wood this weekend. With the gas situation the way it is, it is very difficult to get supplies back and forth.

We have had a couple of rats but they have not tried to eat anything or bite through anything. We have seen "evidence" of their presence and have heard them running around at night. I forgot to bring the rat poison in from town, but the holes have been boarded up with tin so I think we are winning the battle. When Snickers (our cat) comes next week, I think we will conquer the rat battle.

XIX
Shortage, Shortage Everywhere

11 November 1992

Dear Mom and Dad,

We have opted to stay in Ambatoharanana this weekend to get some peace and quiet. Todd and I have to travel back to town tomorrow (Thursday) for a SAFIFI meeting (the evangelism branch of the church). So we will pick up some extra meat and supplies to keep us through the weekend. Todd and I will also travel back into town next Monday for the re-opening of the food program at St. Mark's. At this time they will be feeding 20 children, and the Anglican Sisters will be helping with the "foot work", buying food, cooking distributing, etc.

We are still struggling with the gas shortage and it is becoming increasingly worse for many people. Thankfully, and many thanks to Guy (our friend who works for the gasoline company and has given us gas on many occasions) we have had all we have needed, up to this point. However, we have not done any extra travelling and are still staying close to home. We are still waiting for the trash men to come up the hill and take away the many weeks of trash that has accumulated near our path. It is now crawling down the hill towards our house, and near the top there is so much trash only one person can pass through at a time! When our cooking and hot water "gas" run out, it will be much of a challenge, as we do not have any friend who can get us some!

We have once again stocked up on supplies such as rice, sugar, flour, milk, etc. as we prepare for more shortages. The elections are coming up on Wednesday November 25th. At this point there are 8 people running for election, including the first woman ever to run.

XX
Daddy Nickels is No More

19 November 1992

Dear Mom and Dad,

Things are busy because of the death of "Daddy Nickels", who was 75 years old. He had a stroke and never recovered. He died on Tuesday.

Therefore, our house, this time in Ambatoharanana, is filled with people, most of them family members of Daddy Nickels who are staying on the "other side" of the wing. It makes for a lot of noise, even through the night since the Malagasy custom is to have an "all night wake." Coffee is served, along with small snacks such as bread. Most of the time during the wake is filled with prayers, meditations and singing – a lot of singing – to keep everybody awake! (Maybe that is why it is called "a wake"!) Todd and I did not stay all night – only a couple of hours, until around 10:00. Today is the funeral, with the wrapping of the body first. Unlike in the States, all the people partake in the wrapping and preparation of the body for the funeral.

Monday afternoon is the meeting of my women's group. Duvall is going to teach embroidery from 4:00 to 5:30. Then we will have a short break for tea, and Bible study Prayer time, until about 7:00 p.m.

I have also been asked to teach "pre-school" to the children of the students at Ambatoharanana. There are only a few (about 7) children not in school already so it would not be too much of a hassle and would be good for Corbi and Charese to be with some other children and make some friends. I am preparing a "school room", downstairs in the house in which we are living.

XXI
A Chicken for a Laugh

2 December 1992

Dear Mom and Dad,

Todd and I are in a "rut" because we realize that the "honeymoon" is over and "we are not on vacation" but "we're here to live!" At first we weren't discouraged about the language because we were surprised at how many people spoke English. But now we realize the importance of learning the national language and we also know how difficult it is. I've picked it up fairly well because I learn many times by listening. Todd, on the other hand, learns by visual means and needs to be in a "school setting" to learn. We may have to cut down on other activities and be more involved in language learning. Please pray about our areas of direction and involvement. There is so much and the possibilities are endless, and they are all "good" areas to be working with. So pray that God will give us direction and that we will be led by Him.

Todd has a desire of travelling to various churches leading evangelism conferences, which is a challenge because the roads are so bad. Travelling is neither easy nor fast!

I have a desire to be working with churches, as they have no Christian Education program. Once again, I was outside the church building on Sunday morning since Charese wanted to run around and play instead of listen to the Bishop's sermon in Malagasy. The churches do not have nursery or Sunday school during service. So, many times there are children and parents outside. Yesterday, at one time, I counted over 40 people outside the church building during service!

We have a new family member; her name is "Mauve," meaning purple. She is a chicken! It was given to us this weekend by the priest and his wife. There is a Malagasy custom that if a person makes your children laugh for the first time, they owe that person a chicken. Strange! So, we have a chicken.

XXII
We Walked ... And Walked ... And Walked

2 December 1992

Dear Betsy,

I received your letter postmarked October 20th and Mom's letter postmarked November 20th on the same day – yesterday! The mail system is always interesting. Still have not received the package that St. David's sent us, but did receive a letter, Saturday, from Phil Zampino—postmarked August 2, 1991!

Yesterday, I went up to my "meditation point", the rock up on the hill behind our house in Ambatoharanana. I walked up there with Bible, journal and a cushion in a bag, but placed my things there because I wanted to take a walk and get some exercise first. Exercise I did, and returned two and one-half hours later! Just when I had begun my walk I met up with two students' wives (and one of their workers, carrying baby on back) who were going a "little far to buy rice." I have not really learned what a "little far" in Malagasy terms is, but they did inform me that it was a "walk." So, since I wanted to get exercise, I decided to go along with them. They, of course, were thrilled because it is not often that that would be done, and we could also talk about the women's program to be started at the school. I thought it would be a good chance to get to know the women (one of the student's wives is new this year) and also to practice my Malagasy.

So, we walked, and walked, and walked…and in a little less than an hour later we reached our destination. The villagers were very surprised to see a white *vazaha* in shorts, and gave us all a warm welcome. We were asked into their homes and stayed half an hour at the marketplace. After the buying of rice and *voanjobory* (a nut, like chickpeas, that is used as *laoka)* I began to wonder how all this rice was going to get back to Ambatoharanana, another hour's walk home. They looked at me, a little startled, for of course they were going to carry the 100-kilo sack of grain on their heads and walk the hour home!

XXIII
He Counted Four Stars

15 January 1993

Dear Mom and Dad, Betsy, Ken and the boys,

Thank you so much for the keyboard! How wonderful and practical at the same time!

I am continually reminded about the extremely low academic level, not only among the students, but even more so among their wives. On Wednesday, our first day of preschool, the children and I were learning each other's names, writing their names on the board and making name tags. I asked the mothers to come the first day so that the children would not be afraid (many times village children are afraid of white people). Anyway, I asked the children their names and asked the mothers the spelling of the names. And, one of the mothers did not even know how to spell her child's name! This amazed me because Corbi can already spell (without help) and write "CORB"!

I thought I would start the children on something funny, but basic, that is cutting their nametags out from a pattern of a bear. It was not a small bear, but a decent size for the children to cut. But I soon realized that all of the children did not know how to use scissors! Of course not, I reminded myself that they probably do not own any!

One thing is certain. I will not have many "scrap" left over from class. After the children's mothers cut out the bear nametags I noticed they did not "scrap" the paper, but eyed the ordinary construction paper very carefully, to see what I was going to do with it. When I asked them if they wanted to take it home, they were more than eager. Then, to put the icing on top of the cake, I let each child pick one crayon to take home and keep! They thought it was like Christmas! (And we have a couple of boxes of "24" that Charese eats! Are we not blessed?)

Yesterday I was reading a book. I translated a very simple English book into Malagasy words, and asked the oldest student (5 years old) to count the stars. This youngster seemed relatively bright and eager to learn. After all, he could cut with scissors the second day, after I taught him how to use them. I was curious to find out how high he could count and he reached an astonishing 4! Well, one thing I can say for this preschool, there are lots of things to teach these kids!

Charese joined pre-school. No difference in ability – only age.

XXIV
Did She See a Map ... Or a Ghost?

17 February 1993

Dear Mom and Dad,

Corbi and Charese are watching Sesame Street video (for the 25th time).

Teaching pre-school certainly is a challenge. I am not sure which is more of a challenge, teaching the children or teaching the women who are helping me teach the children. It is amazing how much these grown ladies with children do not know themselves. Today, I started to teach the children geography for I have a different country to study for the next fifteen or so lessons. I started today with Madagascar and posted a map of the world and a map of Madagascar on the wall of our classroom. The children and I sat on a straw mat right by the map to get a good view. I do not think the helper had EVER seen a map of the world before today! When I was explaining some bits of geography I struggled for some Malagasy words and when I asked my helper, she either had no idea and looked at me speechless, or it was like a light finally went on in her brain, and she learned something for the first time herself. When I showed her a map her eyes popped out as if she had seen a ghost and she was definitely very attentive in the lesson I had for the 3-5 year olds!

We have so many learning tools in the states that we never even think of them as learning tools. For example, all the children's toys can be learning tools. Take a road map for instance; the average American has probably at least two or three road maps in the car and a world atlas at home. Plus, road maps are sold everywhere – at grocery stores, at gas stations. 7–11's etc...and are in most places of learning – libraries, classrooms, even in many churches (who have missionaries) But here in Madagascar, I have only seen two places which carry road maps, one being the map makers, and the other one at "Denny's" (The restaurant/diner where the kids ate ice-cream everyday for breakfast) in Fianarantsoa. That makes two places, which sold maps in all of our travels for the one and a half years we have been here!

I also realize how blessed I am to have had so many experiences. I am by no means yet a world traveler, but I have been able to see a few places, and different countries…Mexico, South America, Puerto Rico, Jamaica, Canada, Holland, Israel and now Madagascar. To think that most of these students and their families came from rural villages, and have not seen Antananarivo, their own capital City even once. To think that the transportation is so horrible in this country that it would take longer to drive to Ft. Dauphin where we spent Christmas than to fly back to the states and arrive at your house!

When I get lonely or feeling sorry for myself, I just think of the many students and their families who have made sacrifices in their lives as well. Many of them have traveled for weeks, on rustic taxi-busses.

XXV
Free to be a Woman

18 February 1993

Dear Mom and Dad, Betsy and Ken, and Great Gran,

Believe it or not, and sometimes I cannot believe it myself, I really LIKE missionary life! Before coming out to the "field" I though that missionary life was something that I might dread. But that certainly was a misconception! I am really surprised that I do not get lonely more often. In fact, I am hardly lonely at all! Being lonely is different than missing people. Certainly I miss you guys, Mom and Dad, and other church friends. But I know there will be a day when we can all be together again, and therefore I look ahead to those days instead of drowning myself in self-pity. And I have found the weapon against loneliness in my relationship with two people— God and Todd.

First, my relationship with God has to be consistent. I find that I HAVE to sit down and read the Bible and write in my journal. If I do not, I am a totally different (and irritable) person! Writing in my journal helps me to reflect upon yesterday's or today's thoughts and feelings. It helps me to learn from my mistakes and it is a form of communication – like talking to a friend. Many times it is a real self-discipline to write, but it always is worth the effort! And, of course, you know all the benefits of reading the Bible. Need I mention all the peace and contentment that it brings?

Secondly, my relationship with Todd has to be good. Todd is my best friend here in Madagascar, and he will have to remain so. I cannot rely on relationships with other missionaries, although I do enjoy these relationships. But to rely on these would be putting too much dependence on another person, and I also have to be careful that I do not put too much dependence on Todd. But, friendships are not easy to form. Since we live out in the village – over an hour away from any other missionaries – it is not just like I can stop by when I feel like it! And, I cannot just pick up the phone to see how someone is doing or to pass the time when I feel blue. Therefore, I have had to become extra dependent upon God for my peace and contentment. It has been fun to be so close to Todd and the children. I feel our relationship has really benefited from moving out here to the village. We are a very close family, not only physically, since we live in only a couple of rooms, but also emotionally. I think it is healthy and we are not too dependent upon each other. Having pre-school for the children helps also because they have other friends to play with when they want.

So, I think I am changing. In the states, I used to be an extrovert getting my strength through relationships and from people. It seemed I always had to be doing something or seeing someone! But here in Madagascar I think I am changing to an introvert. I get my strength from being alone, from taking long walks or jogging in the country, from reading a book or writing a letter. I really like this life in the country and I praise God for the changes He has brought in our ministry.

I like the pre-school on Wednesday and Friday mornings, but I especially like the Children's Church on Wednesdays at 3:00 p.m. This is a very evangelical time, just telling the children about the love of God. What a joy it is to teach children because they are so free to express themselves. Indeed, Jesus' words are true that we are all to become like children if we want to see the Kingdom of God. These children (average 60) are so eager to learn about God, and they like the fact that sometime I bring paper and crayons to make small little crafts! Yesterday we talked about the Good Samaritan and then made "little hands". Each person traced his or her hand and then we wrote on the hand, *Mila mpanampy ve ianao?* (Do you need a helper?) Then we taped them onto their shirt and they wore it home – helping them to remember to be a Good Samaritan at home, at school, and in everyday life!

I feel like I am becoming the woman that God has designed me to be. I feel free to be who I am, free to break out of any molds, expectations or cultures that other people might try to place on me. Truly this is a freedom experience! For example: in the village, it is relatively UNHEARD of that women participate in sports. I have NEVER seen a woman (or for that fact, even a man) running for pleasure. But this is something that is very important for my physical, mental, emotional, and spiritual well being. So, it was either break out of the cultural expectations and be myself, or suffer for it! So, I decided to break out of the mold and be free in Christ! The exciting part is that people love it!! When I jog down the path the villagers stop, stare, and wait for me to pass by. It is like I am the queen of England, coming down the street to attend an important inaugural ball! I have told other missionary women and they are dumbfounded! One missionary said to me "So nobody sees you doing this, right?" WRONG!! Whole villages see me, because if one person sees me, they call their friends and say: "Look at the *vazaha* (white person)," and words are shouted like a pile of dominos falling on top of another. But you know what? I feel free in Christ to do whatever I please, as long as it brings honor and glory unto Him. I have to be who God designed me to be, to be my full potential in Christ or I will go crazy!

XXVI
Rain, Rain, Go Away!

2 March 1992

Dear Mom and Dad, Betsy and Ken, and Great Gran,

What a gloomy day – therefore a great day to sit down at the computer and write you all a letter. It is raining…and raining…and raining… I do not know how Noah and his wife could stand all those days on the ark and all they saw was RAIN! How did they keep their children (although they were not the ages of two and almost four) and their animals happy? A cyclone hit the Eastern coast above Tamatave yesterday. Days before the cyclone hit we had rain…and today we have rain…and they predict more rain for days to come. I will be very happy when the dove comes back with an olive branch in its mouth!

You would have laughed with me yesterday when I went out for a little jog. You see, I just HAD to get out of the house because I had been sitting all day at the computer, inputting information for Todd's classes this semester and my class next semester. I have to prepare in advance for my Christian Education class next semester because I will not have an interpreter in class, but rather will have my notes translated into Malagasy and lecture off my notes. Anyway, I had to get out and there was a "break" in the rain so I put on my jogging shoes and started up the hill behind our house. Good thing I went UP the hill, because when I reached the top, I noticed a large sheet of rain coming my way! And, as the picture on my last note showed, the rain many times comes fast and hard and all at once, not too much unlike the hot, summer rains in Southern Florida! I continued just a minute or two until I figured I really might be stretching the limit and the joys of going for a short jog did not overstate the pains of a broken ankle which might be the result of slipping in the mud and rain on the way home. Consequently, back down the hill I ran (this time a bit faster!) telling everybody on the way: "run, the rain is coming." They were not able to see the rain, because it was up over the hill. I met Fara and Charese on the path by the house and as soon as I said, "Come quick, the rain is coming," it gave us a brief warning of very hard, but not too many, rain drops. Then, the minute we all stepped foot on the porch the DOWNPOUR came! Fortunately none of us were really wet, and I continued my exercises upstairs in our room from cassette tapes.

The heavy rains made me think that perhaps Todd and Corbi might not make it back from town. It was a father/daughter day of running errands, going to the supermarket, stopping at the British Embassy to pick up a check for ONE MILLION Malagasy Francs (not US dollars), and they donated another refrigerator to hold medicines at the second dispensary. Going to the post office to pick up Todd's birthday present, which arrived, unharmed and very well liked, etc... Todd also had a meeting regarding the feeding program at St. Mark's church and signing contracts, etc. for the second dispensary to open in three months. A doctor and an administrator have been hired, and they begin their three months "internship" soon. Anyway, the road is getting pretty bad and when it rains it either becomes a mud hole or a streambed. But the rain finally slowed

down to a hard drizzle, and Todd and Corbi returned home at around
7:15 pm, after a very busy day with no mishaps.

XXVII
The Humbling Bucket Shower

26 March 1993

Dear Mom and Dad,

I am having fun jogging. The fun part is that there is not any
traffic that I have to dodge, but just a bunch of cows that are coming
home from pasture! Literally, this is the only thing I have to stop for
and it makes me laugh each time. The people are amused at me and
always remark about my strength. It amazes them that someone would
want to jog for pleasure when they work so hard in their fields all
day. Many people remark that it is so good to jog because it makes
me so BIG in the HIPS…to be big is a sign of wealth to them and
they think they are giving me the highest compliment when they say
I am very big in the hips!! Here I am running for exercise so that I
am not so big in the hips. Humility is certainly good for the soul!

General cleaning of dishes is always a chore since one has to
boil the water first, get out the buckets, and fetch the water from the
river. Taking a "bucket shower" when I have finished exercising is
also humbling for the soul.

XXVIII
The $ 7.50 that Built the Church

15 April 1993

Dear Mom and Dad,

We had a missionary potluck and picnic on Easter Monday out here in Ambatoharanana and over 60 missionaries (children included) from all denominations came! It really was a good turnout and we had lots of fun playing volleyball, croquet, taking walks and having an Easter Egg Hunt for the kids.

Today was a very unique and fun day. Corbi and Charese and I went to visit a neighboring village (from Ambatoharanana), which is about 25 minute walk (45 with the kids). Naina, the student/driver of the Land Rover, is from this village and he and his family are staying out here during the Easter break. He and Giselle came to pick me and the kids up (we were not expecting them, of course they could not call first, and I was in the middle of baking bread) to take us to their village. Truly it was a wonderful experience. We got some good exercise (Corbi and Charese both wanted to be carried all the way back; Naina and another student carried them and helped us make it home). The whole village was so excited to have visitors! Of course they do not get many visitors, much less "Vazaha".

Naina's family (father, mother, grandfather, grandmother, brothers, etc...) was all there to welcome us and offered us warm milk (which was fresh from their cow, and still warm after being boiled – good thing!) and bread. Then they took us to see the very small Anglican church which is in the center of their village, which consisted about ten houses, two of which were their families!). We went in and saw the very simple building and then one by one many of the parishioners came greet me. Each one thanked me (and Todd) for providing the funds to finish the roof on their church. The old roof was very worn and had fallen in and they were just $7.50 short of completion when they came to ask Todd and I if they could borrow the money to fix the roof. Todd and I were so taken aback by the fact that 1) they wanted to borrow the money and did not ask to have it, 2) they only needed 7.50 to fix it, and 3) they had paid for all the previous work themselves. We gave them the necessary funds and told them it was a gift and they did not have to return it. Today it was such a joy for me to go and see the roof completed, but even more so, to know of their heart felt gratitude. Truly these people were thrilled with our very small gift, which was not small in their eyes. To see their sincere gratitude was truly worth the sweat of the brow due to the walk up and down hills and through rice paddies. (I fell in twice and came home with very muddy feet and shoes!)

I came back from Naina's village with *voan-dalana* (fruit from the road) such as a large bunch of garlic (Naina's father is a farmer, obviously, and there are no corporations in his area!), fresh cow's milk and two fruits I had never seen, nor eaten before. One was a type of tomato, which grows on a large tree (Persimmon) and the other a large orange fruit, which is so hard to describe that I won't even try! Of course the children were thrilled to eat the sweet fruits. The gift of thanks from the church was a live chicken, which I carried under my arm all the way home (when I was not carrying Corbi on my back). What thrilled Naina's family the most was that Charese did not want to leave and when we asked her if she wanted to go home she would shake her head, say "No," and re-close and lock the gate so nobody could get out! They loved it!

Yes, you might have caught in the above paragraph that I was baking bread this morning! Yes, for the first time in my 33 years of life, I baked three loaves of white bread. I guess that is what one does in the country if they want to eat bread! Certainly there is no place to buy it! We had not expected to stay out here in Ambatoharanana this long, and we had also not expected to have visitors stay with us so long. Therefore, we had been running out of food and were scraping everything possible from the cupboard. This morning I decided that if we wanted to eat that I better bake some bread. It started as whole wheat but then found out that we were out of whole-wheat flour and it could not be something so simple as banana bread, or a "quick bread" because we did not have any eggs or bananas! So I HAD to make a "real" bread with yeast and all! Much to my amazement it turned out pretty tasty. I guess so, considering the fact that this morning I baked three loaves, and by the evening there was only one left! When he returned from the city that night, Todd was amazed to find a freshly baked bread on the table. In fact, he absolutely sure his wife never baked it. I had never baked any bread before and he was convinced that it was our houseguests who made it!

XIX
Our First Funeral in Madagascar

18 June 1993

Yesterday a 16-year old boy died. This was shocking to me. 16 year old boys do not just die like that in the States, unless if by an accident or through some severe sickness. But here, one day the boy was fairly healthy, and two days later, he was dead. Rumor has it that he consumed some medicine given to him by a witch doctor. Rev. Flaurent said that this rumor could very well be true. He visited the doctor at the dispensary three times on Wednesday, which was a holiday, but there was nothing that Dr. Zoë could do. And the next day, he died. This is all so strange to me, definitely out of my culture.

I went to visit the mourning mother and other family members with three of the student's wives yesterday, just hours after the boy had died. The family lives right in the village of Ambatoharanana. It is said that it is probably in this village where they consulted the witch. I just found out that Ambatoharanana is known for its witches.

Anyway, yesterday morning at 11:00 we went to offer our condolences to the family. Before going to their house, we met briefly to discuss what we were going to say, who was going to read Psalm 90, and who would lead in prayer. There were three things to say and four people volunteered, which meant that I did not have to say a word. I was glad about that. It was, of course, all in Malagasy! After our brief discussion, the four of us walked down the path and across the dirt road to the small, dark, brick house with only two windows in which lived the bereaved family. Straw mats covered the floor like carpeting would cover the floors of the homes in America and there was no furniture in the three small rooms except a wobbly bench that would barely fit three of us, and a table on which the boy's body was placed, covered with mosquito netting. Next to the boy's body was a flickering candle, put there out of respect for the boy rather than for lighting purposes, even though there is no electricity in the village.

In walked behind the first of the student wives, Madame Victorine, followed by Madame Noro and Madame Rodine. I was hardly at the front door when I heard a very loud wailing coming from the next room. Perhaps it was the mother mourning over the death of her young boy, I thought. However when I walked in the room I saw Madame Victorine leaning over the boy's body, wailing at the top of her lungs. This surprised me because there was not even a tear in her eye just minutes before!

The boy's mother, along with the grandmother and two aunts were placidly sitting on the floor against the brick wall one beside the other, knees close to their chests, with a blanket covering their bodies and their heads. Their eyes were misty, but they did not wail, for this mourning time was for the visitors, or so it seemed. After a couple of minutes of wailing, the boy's grandmother asked Madame Victorine to stop. And that was that. No more crying, no more wailing, no more misty eyes.

Oh, there is the church bell. It has rung three times to proclaim a funeral. I will go now.

3:10 p.m. I just arrived back from the funeral about an hour ago. Ambatoharanana and all the villages surrounding Ambatoharanana seem to be sober. The land is quiet. The funeral was certainly sad. People from many surrounding villages came. First there was a church service. The church was filled with villagers, normally not churchgoers, barefoot yet wearing their best clothes, which were dirty and filled with holes. But their clothes did not matter to them. What they had, they wore. The important thing to them was to be there to support the family. The preacher, a student in his final year who will graduate next month, spoke on the passage from John. "Do not be sad in your hearts. Believe in God, believe also in me." It was a powerful sermon—from what I could understand of course, and I prayed that many of the people's hearts were touched.

After the church service we all progressed by foot to the family tomb. The Cross-bearer walked first, followed by the students dressed in their cassocks, then the family members and then friends. The family tomb was about a ten-minute walk, just on the hillside to the south of Ambatoharanana. The tomb was opened and ready to receive the boy's body, along with the other family members and ancestors. The most difficult part, emotionally, was to see the boy's body, wrapped up in a white shroud, taken out of the coffin and placed into the tomb. At this point there was much wailing (there was not any in the church) by most of the family members, and the men seemed to hold back the women from desiring to touch the boy's body one last time. Finally, the family formed a receiving line to thank all the people for coming. As I shook their hands, I silently prayed for each one. It really was very sad, but definitely an interesting cultural experience for me.

I write all this to you, not to depress you, nor to scare you about the fact of witches and witchdoctors in our neighboring village, but rather to help you know about everyday village life in a country in which many people still hold to the traditional ancestral worship and animism. The spiritual warfare is among us, right in this place where the college is located. It is real and hard, but nothing that our Lord Jesus Christ has not already claimed the victory over! As the old hymn goes, "Onward Christian Soldiers, marching on to WAR!" Yes, we are in a battle and the battle is real. But is not it comforting to know that we have ALREADY WON! We just have to be faithful and fight in intercessory prayer and by spreading the Word of God! Please be in prayer with us.

XXX
Dispensary Number Two

June 1993

Dear All,

DISPENSARY NUMBER TWO OPENS!

On June 19th we had the great privilege of opening the second dispensary for the Anglican Church in Madagascar. 300 people gathered for this event at St. Mark's Church in Tsinjohasina (the site of the feeding program for twenty five orphans), a rural village located about fifteen miles outside Antananarivo. This has been a lot of work for Todd to coordinate but Bishop Remi and the Anglican parishioners are truly excited about the growth in social development of the Anglican Church.

The dispensary at Ambatoharanana is going very well. For the first six months of this year it has remained self-supporting, which is our goal in whatever programs we initiate. The patient average intake has doubled and is currently at about 200 patients weekly. To date, the dispensary has cared for over 3,000 patients since the opening in May 1992. Free vaccinations are given on the third and fourth Thursdays of every month.

Unfortunately, the average age of the Malagasy population has dropped from 21 years of age to 18 years. One can really see the need for these dispensaries! We really appreciate the donation of 3,000 English pounds given by the Diocese of Canterbury (Britain) and used toward the opening of this second Anglican dispensary.

XXXI
Whoa Boy ...Hot Dogs with Heinz!

4 July 1993

Dear Mom and Dad,

Today was the American Ambassador's formal luncheon with all the dignitaries. Truly a lovely celebration and Todd and I were thrilled to be part of it. The informal family picnic is on Saturday at the marine house. Corbi is looking forward to eating HOT DOGS with HEINZ 57! She ate four last year. We refuse to buy them because they are the most expensive meat available, even more costly than chicken and ham! Of course the ketchup is flown over and sold (only for embassy employees) at the commissary. Fireworks will blast off at 6:00 p.m. One of the embassy employees flew all the way over to Mauritius to purchase them! There will be sack races and games for the kids, along with volleyball, softball, tennis and swimming.

XXXII
Oh Lord, Not Malaria Again

July 1993

Dear Mom, Dad, Great Gran, Betsy, Ken and the Boys,

I am recovering from malaria. It is my second bout with the disease and it is certainly not a fun fight! It came on so suddenly last Wednesday night, after Wilma and I had just taken a walk to a "neighboring village" to buy some tomatoes. She and her two girls drove for one hour to Ambatoharanana, where they spent the night. Craving for pizza, we walked the round trip of one hour and fifteen minutes to buy the necessary ingredients. We could not imagine pizza without tomatoes!

Soon after I was taken down by fever. With the help of Tylenol every four hours, my fever was kept between 101 ^{0}F-102 ^{0}F. At first, I thought it was a bad, winter flu. But after Sunday night's attack with chills and shakes, followed by a fever of 104 ^{0}F, I changed my mind. I cooled myself with cold liquids and compresses and took six tablets of Chloroquine. Since then, I have been getting steadily better with only one slight shake and fever attack of slightly over 100 ^{0}F. Now I need bed rest to recover completely.

This must be a relapse of last year's bite, still in my bloodstream. Being the end of the school year, my defenses are down. However, this time it was not as bad, because I did not have the upset stomach with vomiting and diarrhea.

XXXIII
Fois Gras at Hilton

24 July 1993

Greetings to the family!

This weekend was special. As a gift, we were given a free weekend at the Madagascar Hilton – usually it costs $190 per night! Of course the service was very nice and the General Director set up a bottle of red wine, an assorted cheese tray and the infamous *fois gras* (duck's liver) served with toast. It was awaiting us in our room.

XXXIV
Too Complicated Cooking

31 July 1993

Greetings!

After two years of being in Madagascar, Todd is working on the installation of the washing machine, together with the Administrator, David. Nothing is easy here in Madagascar. Todd and I have been waiting for three days for people to show up and give us estimates on the cost.

At the same time, we hooked-up the washer and we will hopefully install the hot water heater and get hot water in the bathroom (including the sink!) Until this happens, we have borrowed a 3-burner gas stove from the Bishop. This really helps out and now we do not have to light the charcoal just to make tea or warm-up leftovers!

Some people wonder why I do not like to cook! Perhaps because it is too complicated here!

XXXV
A Car ... A Car ... My Kingdom for a Car!

23 September 1993

Dear Mom and Dad,

Our car broke down and now we need a new alternator and two other parts of which they only have ONE of here in Madagascar. Along with the fact that only one piece is available, the three pieces are very expensive (one piece amounting to almost $400.00). In the meantime, we are looking for someone to hand-carry the piece back and forth to the States.

Todd is leaving for the rainforest on Sunday. I will stay in town with the kids. To get into town, we have to walk for forty minutes to catch the "taxi-buses". Corbi and Charese walk the three and a half miles and we carried some clothes, books and the fifteen-pound car alternator!

Todd will take the taxi-buses to Moramanga; then walk 71 kilometers to Anosibe An'Ala. From there he and the Bishop will travel from parish to parish for another week. He will be gone for one or two weeks and is very much looking forward to this adventure. While he is gone I will prepare my women's Bible studies (in Malagasy), which I lead once a week, and also prepare my lesson plans for the children's pre-school, twice a week. School begins in less than a month!

SOMA's Australian Director, John Wyndham, checked on round the world air tickets - $1,700! Perhaps when we fly home to the States we will fly around the world!

XXXVI
Mrs. McGregor? Or Mrs. Socialite?

23 September 1993

Dear Betsy,

I had a wonderful time with you during your visit. I cried and cried on Wilma's shoulder after you left. She told me that she was going to pray specifically that I would not be depressed, but rather Praise God for the opportunity of having you here! I am so thankful to God that He answered my prayer for a "miracle" and Aunt Adele sent you over to visit me! It was so much fun to have you both! It makes such a difference now, to know that when I write about certain things, you can understand and picture those things I write about. Praise God for His faithfulness!

Since you left, Todd has been traveling. At the end of August he traveled for six hours by car on a very bad road...impassible during the rainy season. He went to a small village called Faratsiho to look at an area to build a third dispensary. This would be a good area since there is already a building and an Anglican school, but no medical facilities to speak of for several kilometers. The only problem would be transportation of medicines. As I said, the road is terrible, and during the rainy season the only way to get medicines in would be to fly them in by helicopter or airdrop them by plane. At this time there is no helicopter available in Madagascar, but the missionary organization, "Mission Aviation Fellowship", hopes to get one in the next couple years, specifically to help out in situations like these.

While Todd is away I am playing Mrs. "Socialite". Thanks be to God, I have made some very good friends this past year. One is a dear friend in Christ. She and her husband are missionaries with the Assemblies of God Church. They have two children. Wilma is one with whom I can pray, laugh, cry and share all kinds of "missionary struggles and adventures." I thank God for bringing us together. It has really been an answer to prayer. As David had a heart-to-heart friend, she is my "Jonathan".

God has also given me some friends outside of our "Christian Community." Todd and I have become friends with the Peace Corps Director, Bob Freidman his wife, Cheryl and their three children. Corbi and Charese also find it refreshing to play with American friends and speak English. Cheryl and Bob play tennis (quite well!). While Todd is gone, we are going to get together, play tennis and the girls and I will even spend the night at their house (a good plan since our car has broken down!).

Todd and I had the British Ambassador (Peter Smith) and his wife out to our home in Ambatoharanana to see the dispensary and school grounds. The British Embassy donated some funds that were used toward buying a refrigerator for the dispensary. The Ambassador's wife, Suzanne, and I hit it off. She has asked me to call her while Todd is away. She wants to get together for lunch or go on a picnic to the zoo with the children. I think she really misses her three children and three grandchildren! So, even though I do not really like the times that Todd is away, I try to make the best of them. I thank God that He has given me friends. Last year at this time I would not have had so many. This certainly has been an answer to prayer!

Personally I feel refreshed and renewed, spiritually and physically. The girls and I went on a four day mini-vacation to the beach (not ocean, but inland lake) with the MAF pilot and family, Emil and Margrit Kundig, and their four children, Tiffany, Timon, Tabitha and Tobias. Tabitha, is a good friend of Corbi's. She is six, that is one year older than Corbi. It was a great vacation for all of us.

Spiritually I feel renewed due to a three-day fast, which the Lord led me to do. Believe me, it was not MY idea not to eat for three days! Anyway, I had some wonderful prayer time with the Lord and I feel SO refreshed. It has been nine years since my last fast and now I realize how much I have missed out.

XXXVII
Todd Earns a $ 6.00 Massage

9 October 1993:

Greetings to the family!

Todd just arrived back from the rainforest last night at around 6:00 p.m. He had a marvelous time! Moments of his rainforest experience are indescribable, he said, and even though it was difficult (they walked over 140-150 kilometers!) it was a very worthwhile experience, to say the least. I am anxious to see the video Todd took. Todd said one of the most moving experiences was to see the villagers welcome the Bishop. They walk for miles on end to meet the Bishop and when they finally saw him, they began to sing a particular song, sung only for the Bishop, at the top of their lungs. Todd said it almost brought tears to his eyes. He is now getting a massage, worth every bit of the $6.00 per hour!

XXXVIII
Its Holy, Pronounced as-Uli, which Means Holy

26 October 1993

Greetings from Madagascar!

Our house has expanded – we now occupy five rooms instead of three! Now we have a living room, our own bedrooms and a guest room. It is nice for Corbi and Charese to "stay put" when we have visitors.

Suzanne Smith, the British Ambassador's wife came out to Ambatoharanana just to "chat and visit". We had a nice time. She came in shorts and we just relaxed, took a long walk, ate shepherds pie for lunch and she left at around 2:30. Next time she comes she wants to bring Rosemarie Barrett, the American Ambassador's wife with her. Rosemarie comes back from home leave in a couple of weeks. Suzie tells me they are very good friends.

The Ambatoharanana library is looking good! Renovations are almost complete, thanks to the United Thank Offering donation. Pictures enhance the décor, books are in order, and the financial donation used to buy furniture gives students a nice place to relax and read.

Tomorrow we are going on a mini-vacation to a small village south of Tamatave with the Bishop and Elisabeth. Holy and Eugene have a "vacation spot" at this village and on Saturday they are having a consecration of a new chapel they built. They asked us to come, and since we do not have a car we asked the Bishop if we could ride along in his (and split the cost of gas).

XXXIX
Madagascar ... What's in a Name

31 October 1993

Greetings from roadside!

We are on our way back to Tana, after a very nice three-day vacation with Bishop Remi and Elizabeth. After crossing the one lane bridge at Brickaville (an additional lane for the railroad), then we took a rough 22-kilometer road to the Pangalane canal. There we boarded a "ferry". Similar to the raft used by Tom Sawyer, it was built out of 15 logs tied together. The limit is 3 cars. Sometimes people have to wait for the second load, depending on the weight of the vehicles and passengers! After crossing the canal, there is a lovely spot – a peninsula surrounded by either ocean on one side or fresh water (so clean and so clear!) There was no need for running water or a hot shower (good thing as of course there was not any!) Accommodations were very simple, no electricity, but nice. Our family slept in our tent and Holy had a small hut built for the Bishop and Elizabeth. Of course an outhouse was used instead of a toilet, and the worst thing was when Corbi dropped the pad-lock key for the outhouse down the hole! Good thing the outhouse was just built and had hardly been used. Todd cut a long piece of bamboo and went "fishing" for the key!

Now we are on our way home and what is normally a six and a half hour drive has now become a fifteen-hour drive, and we are still waiting outside of Tana, 55 kilometers away. The Bishop's car broke down at about 5:30 pm. last night – 35 miles East of Moramanga. Luckily, some friends drove by a few minutes later and stopped to help us. Well, we think it was lucky, even though Todd thinks they do not know anything about cars and have "extended our waiting process" by trying! Since we do not have the number for the local AAA, (ha, ha!) the eight of us (four in our family, Bishop, Elisabeth, their daughter and guest from England) slept in the car and went kilometer by kilometer trying to start or restart and fix or re-fix the car. Now we have run out of gas and we are waiting for our friends to come back with gas. We hope they find a gas station open at 6:00 a.m. on a Sunday! We think it would be a good investment to start a branch of the AAA in Madagascar. Maybe that is how MADAGASCAR gets its name—one gets MAD when there is no GAS in the CAR—MADAGASCAR!

XL
Lets Fly with Santa

19 November 1993

Dear Mom and Dad,

Next week we will have seven people in our house in Ambatoharanana (plus our family of four!), the Bishop and a guest from England included. We are housing the ordinands for a retreat. I told them our house may not be suitable for a RETREAT with two pre-school children hanging around all day!

EWM suggests a special request letter for finances or we will have to come off of the mission field and raise support!

I was talking to Fara about the bad news concerning our car and the expense and duration of time that it would take to get our car alternator. I was explaining to her that we now do not know how we are going to get to Betroka to spend Christmas with the Rheingans, our Lutheran missionary friends. We have been looking forward to this trip for so long, and the kids especially want to play with Paul and Kelly, so we are still trying to work out details.

Anyway, I was telling Fara that we do not know how we are going to get to Betroka, that maybe we would have to take a taxi-bus (a last resort for us with two small children, a two-day drive on horrible roads). Charese was sitting at the table, but playing like a normal three-year-old, and I did not even know that she was listening to our conversation. However, she must have been listening to every word, because she interrupted me to say "Mommy, I know how we can go (to Betroka). Let us fly with Santa Claus!" Both Fara and I looked at Charese and laughed. I smiled at Charese's glimmering blue eyes. She furthered her comment by saying, "He is such a nice man!"

Oh, to have the faith of a child again. Nothing is too difficult, nothing is too hard, nothing is too complicated.

This is another busy week. We have had such a changeover in houseguests that I had to ask the last houseguest to change his own sheets on the bed so the Bishop from the Northern Diocese of Madagascar would have a clean bed to sleep in! Since the guests are most of the time in-town, and we are most of the time in the village. It sometimes becomes a little complicated when new guests come! Oh, well, all houseguests that come to Madagascar seem to be flexible and do not mind doing chores such as changing their own sheets! At least we have enough sheets and towels now (thanks to the shipment and the friends in the states who sent them) to be able to change them without having to wash them first!

XLI
Charlie Says I DO to Nivo

2 December 1993

Dear Mom and Dad,

We hosted the wedding reception of Charlie (American Architect working for MSAADA) and Nivo (woman he met here in Madagascar) - a backyard reception after the church wedding. It was beautiful.

Todd traveled to Faratshio, by "taxi-be" arriving in the middle of a heavy hail storm, which he described as the size of golf balls. Then he took a 14-kilometer walk up and down mountains, checking for an appropriate site for a dispensary. The British Embassy has agreed to give $2,600 toward the next project. Added to the $1,500 from St. Andrews, this will give us a good start. Currently, we are giving out free Nivaquine (malaria medicine). Todd is interviewing potential doctors to work at the dispensary. The target opening date is June 1994.

XLII
Corbi in Black and White

December 1993

Dear Mom, Dad, Great Gran, Betsy, Ken, and of course, the boys,

I really miss worship times in an English-speaking congregation. This week Corbi and Charese will be angels in a Christmas play produced by the American Community at the DM's (second in command, after the ambassador) house.

I guess Corbi and Kevin are getting to the age where they can tell the difference between colors of skin. Just the other day we went to visit some students' wives and play with their children. We sat down on the only hard bench they had in their house...(Big enough to seat two people.) Corbi, after looking at all the people in the room, said to me "Mommy, you and me are the same." I thought to myself, "What does that mean?" and proceeded to ask her. She answered, "We are both white and everyone else is black!"

XLIII
Fort Dauphin

1 January 1994

Dear Mom, Dad, Betsy, Ken, the boy's and Great Gran (and all of our friends who might read this!)

We finally arrived safely at Fort Dauphin with no major mishaps. Some of the public transportation was comfortable (a van like Dad's) in which we had a whole seat to the four of us (we bought four tickets even though Corbi and Charese sat on our laps). On the other hand, some public transportation was quite uncomfortable. The uncomfortable part was day No. 2, from Fianarantsoa to Ihosy (mostly dirty and dusty roads) in the back of a small pick-up truck with sixteen other Malagasy people with children and luggage. That was not a terrifically fun six-hour drive and will make travel in the States for our deputation quite easy!

Betroka is in the middle of nowhere and I think the family will have to undergo quite an adjustment there. Anyway, the Rheingans' car was not big enough for all eight of us. So Todd and Charese, being the good sports that they are, traveled in a large truck (carrying rice, of course), which took eighteen hours to get from Betroka and Ambilambe, a town 50 kilometers West of Fort Dauphin. They left

Betroka on Sunday December 26th at 5:00 a.m. and arrived in Ambilambe at 11:00 p.m. After sleeping through the night in the truck, they took a taxi bus the next morning. They arrived in Fort Dauphin in fairly good time, but then needed to wait for a ride to the peninsula called Lebanon, where the Lutheran mission owns property. Finally they set foot onto the property at 1:30 pm. on Monday the 28th, just a few hours short of two days! Meanwhile, Corbi and I came with the Rheingans and left on Monday morning at 5:30. Steve is a fast driver, (I took car sickness pills the whole way!), and we arrived at 4:15, not even three hours after Todd and Charese! Our trip included stopping at the store to pick up a couple of necessary items! Need I mention the fact that we are all very happy to be flying home!

XLIV
When the Cyclone Hit Us

19 January 1994

Dear All,

We have been hit with lots of rain due to a cyclone. Rains resulted in washing away the road and railroad from here to Tamatave, the coastal city where all the shipments come in. Therefore, gas is once again in shortage since no gas containers can get through. David, the Administrator, spent all day Tuesday waiting in a queue to buy gas!

The road to Ambatoharanana is quite a challenge. The school landrover was unable to pass from Merimandroso through the rice field and up the hill to Ambatoharanana. Todd had to take off his pants and wade through water up to his thighs!

We are having a softball tournament. I am the only woman on all seven teams, including a team from the Japanese Embassy, two Malagasy teams, two American Embassy teams, one from the Mormons, and our missionary team.

XLV
The Strongest Cyclone Bears Down on Us

2 February 1994

Dear All,

We are all gathered downstairs in the "library-cum-office" at 7:30 pm. Why? Just to be cozy? Well, not really. A cyclone is on its way and it is due to hit between Antsirabe and Antananarivo at 12:00 midnight. It is anticipated to be the strongest cyclone in the history Madagascar. The winds are calculated to be between 200 and 300 kilometers an hour, and the span of the storm is 800 kilometers wide, half the size of this island!

We have done all the preparations possible. We have stored water in every container available including a large trash can. We have run last minute errands to the local "7-11" and bought things like matches, candles, bread, biscuits and soup packets. We have moved Fara's, Duvall's and Joseph's belongings from their small room on the side of the house (which lies on the side in the direction of the storm) into the dining room for more security. And we have moved all our mattresses down into Todd's office. Here we wait and pass time listening to the Malagasy radio. Just a couple of hours ago, Fara, Duvall and Joseph "packed" all their belongings. Between the three of them were only a couple of boxes. But Fara and Duvall are still young and single, and have therefore still not accumulated a lifetime of "stuff." But Joseph, a 55-year old married man with four children, packed his life possessions in one small cardboard box. I wonder what could be his treasures in that cardboard box. Perhaps the old pair of tennis shoes that Todd gave him, or the pair of sandals Mom and Dad gave him when they left last year. Those sandals were his first pair of shoes—ever! Or perhaps it is the red pair of St. Andrew's sweatpants, or the sweater, also passed along by Todd. It is amazing to compare our life to Joseph's. If we were to pack up our possessions it would take hours to store them into many boxes. We would even have to pack up two houses (country house and city house)! But simple Joseph, has just to put his few possessions in one small cardboard box. It does cause us to pause and thank God for his blessings and to also remind us to hold on loosely to our possessions for we only have what God has given us in the first place. We are guests in God's world.

XLVI
We Survived!

4 February 1994, 9:45 a.m.

Dear All,

Good news! The cyclone never hit the capital. We had very heavy winds and LOTS of rain but damage was minimal. Parts of our roof leaked and a small part fell in – but nothing major. A house next door collapsed, and a roof was blown off, but besides that, flood damage is the real concern. In Tamatave, however, over 20 are dead and who knows how the road is? As there is only one single road, which leads from the coast to the capital city, this could cause major shortages.

Our power has been out for 15 hours.

XLVII
Living Day by Day

12 February 1994

Greetings again.

Since Tamatave is a major port for the whole country, the cyclone has affected the entire nation. The road was quite heavily damaged in many places, therefore, not allowing the transportation of rice, sugar, and flour, just to name a few supplies. The major shortage is gasoline. The road has been closed for over two weeks. Because of the lack of gasoline, we are unable to bring teachers out to Ambatoharanana. We are literally living day by day, and seeing what God will provide on a daily basis!

The gas shortage has forced me into getting a ride home from the American School (where I am a substitute teacher), with others who live "sort-of" in the same direction. Taxi's are next to impossible to find, and very expensive as they can only be found on the black market. Instead, I ride home with the Italian Ambassador's son in a very luxurious four-wheel all terrain vehicle, complete with ALL the extras. The chauffeur drops me off at a convenient spot from where I can walk home. I teach the Italian Ambassador's son at the American school and now it has paid off from giving them - the Ambassador and his son - private tennis lessons on the side.

XLVIII
Thank Goodness ... The Goodies!

March 1994

Dear Family and Friends at the Chapel of St. Andrews,

Goodness me! Thank you for the kites, tape cleaners, video cassette cleaner, Mickey Mouse glasses, hairbrushes, beach balls, panty hose, HOP ON POP and CAT IN THE HAT, medicine, globe, trial size shampoos, lotions, Barbies and Barbie's clothes, food items, clothing, magazines, etc. sent for Christmas. The gifts you bought way back in July finally arrived and were opened this month! How can we adequately express our thanks?

Todd just arrived back from a four-day hike (100 kilometers) into a remote village where we are building the third Anglican Dispensary. Since the road was cut off by cyclone Geralda, Todd had to walk most of the way on foot. However, the trip was necessary, and if he were to wait until the road was fixed, he may never get there! The roof is almost finished and the health clinic is due to open in May or June, after the rainy season is over. If the road is not fixed from the cyclone damage, we will have to transport the medicines and furniture for the dispensary by ox cart.

XLIX
Good Thing Todd's Not Home

22 May 1994

Todd is still trying to fix the car; the part has arrived. The alternator is in but now the battery is dead! It is not as easy as "just charging it up" since it is in Ambatoharanana, and therefore each time something goes wrong it is at least a two-day process. It will be ready to sell on June 1st when new missionaries want to buy it! So, after being used for almost a year, it will be fixed the day before it is actually sold! Ugh!

Todd is negotiating with porters and ox-carts to transport medicines and furniture to the new dispensary. How it will be done? The first 40 kilometers by ox-cart, then six hours by taxi-bus, finally manually over an 18 kilometer stretch (one way). Who knows when he will be home. It all depends upon the availability of supplies, construction of the building, cooperation of the people, willingness of the oxen pulling the wagons, and the weather!

Good thing Todd is not home; there would be "no room at the inn." The children gave up their beds to our guests and are sleeping with me! Many guests continually stop by for a place to stay. We have had non-stop houseguests for three weeks.

The Viennese Ball is planned for June 3rd. Todd is searching for a tuxedo. All Heads of Missions have been invited: Ambassadors, Peace Corps, Unicef, United Nations, Embassy Employees, Directors of banks, and other bigwigs. I guess Cinderella needs to find a fairy godmother to assist her wardrobe.

L
Todd, the Churchman

Dear Friends and Supporters,

We held an evangelism Conference in Fenoarivo from May 4th to 9th. This is how a Christian witnessed to the work of Christ here in Madagascar.

"Life is hard and difficult here in Madagascar. But because of the impact that you have had on my wife and my family [his wife became a believer], this is what I want to do. I want to pay for the electricity of the building which was used for the crusade."

The impact we all have on others in this temporal life will many times go undeclared. But this comment came from the gentleman who let us use his home, his video, and his television, in order to proclaim the good news of Jesus Christ at the six day Evangelism Conference. The students put into practice what they had learned in Todd's Evangelism classes, and the result was that many committed themselves to Jesus Christ as their Lord and Savior.

Todd and Rev. Samitiana (One of Todd's former students who is now a priest, planting a church in the rural areas of Fenoarivo and Alakamisy) have worked side-by-side coordinating an evangelism crusade in which the students and faculty of the St. Paul's College took part. The conviction of the Holy Spirit was present at the Crusade, and we were able to witness to over 1,500 people, 400 of whom made commitments to Christ. We distributed approximately 1,100 tracts of The Four Spiritual Laws in the Malagasy language. Patsy ministered through a "clowning skit" called "The Gift" and many students shared their personal testimonies.

Todd and two students have been following up each Sunday in a nearby village with an open-air Bible Study and Worship Service. However, due to the winter season, last week was too cold to meet outside. What is one to do in the middle of nowhere, where houses are not much bigger than the Land Rover that Todd drove? You guessed it; last week thirty-five shivering bodies squeezed into the college's Land Rover for the two-hour Bible Study and Worship time! Even though it was so cold outside (the Malagasy custom is to stay in bed when it is cold), these people had such a hunger and thirst to sing and listen to God's word. The exciting point is that most of them have committed themselves to Christ, and now they want to be baptized and serve the Lord!

The Anglican Church is stirring with excitement over the arrival of the Archbishop of Canterbury on June 4th. His three-day visit is something we are all looking forward to!

We want to thank you for your support. Certainly you are People-Reaching-People with us here in Madagascar!

LI
The Archbishop of Canterbury Visits

4 June 2003

Dear Friends and Supporters,

THE ARCHBISHOP OF CANTERBURY"S VISITS!

We have spent the last 30 plus years of our lives in America and never once have we had the opportunity to meet a Presiding Bishop or an Archbishop. However, in the first six months of 1993 we have had the honor of meeting two Archbishops (from Canada and the Indian Ocean) and the Archbishop of Canterbury himself. We have also had the honor of hosting lunch for two of these very honorable guests! Meeting three out of the total of twenty-nine Archbishops in the Anglican Communion has been quite exciting for us!

The climax was to have the Archbishop of Canterbury here in Antananarivo for three days. His arrival on Friday evening was well prepared and touching. The airport was filled with people awaiting the arrival of the Archbishop to give him a warm Malagasy welcome. That they did. The airport parking lot was filled with people from all walks of life, from V.I.P.'s brought by chauffeurs, to barefoot country villagers who had to walk many miles just hoping for a chance to touch the Archbishop's hand. As crowds flocked to see him, it reminded us of the masses who followed Jesus, and what a strenuous life the Archbishop must lead.

Many of the youth, wearing their scout uniforms, were there, either playing in the band, or waving their paper flags picturing the Archbishop. One could hardly recognize that the airport was in Madagascar. The chandeliers and big, soft chairs in the V.I.P. section must have been imported, and the large room had all the trimmings, including soldiers dressed up in handsome red uniforms which looked straight from a story book. The red carpet was laid for the Archbishop and his wife, who traveled along with two other representatives from the Diocese of Canterbury. As the Archbishop disembarked from the plane, the skies were illuminated with the strong lights of the Malagasy television cameras. After a brief speech to the press and a longer, but still short speech to the welcoming crowd, the Archbishop was ushered into the British Ambassador's car and led away in a convoy of police and other Embassy vehicles.

Saturday was exciting for the students and faculty of St. Paul's College because the Archbishop took a whole two hours out of his three-day stay just to speak to the students. He gave what we would call a "pep talk" about being in ministry, emphasizing the honor we have to serve God. It was the Archbishop's challenge to us that what we have been called to by God is the Lord's ministry, not ours. He emphasized the importance of lay ministry and the responsibility of the laity with the "successful" church. Among other things, he encouraged us all to be in prayer and be in daily Bible study so that we can keep up our strength in the Lord.

Sunday's service in the garden just outside of the cathedral was beautiful, though it was very cold and windy. The church service included a full procession, of which Todd was a part, down the cathedral steps, across the street, through the park and finally up to the altar. There were many banners of various pictures and colors, which helped to make the whole atmosphere quite beautiful.

Approximately 3,000 people attended the service. We were anticipating a few more, but we think the cold and windy day might have held a few people back. All in all, it was a delightful and very heart-warming weekend.

LII
Todd, the Local Hero

7 June 1994

Dear Mom and Dad, Betsy, Ken and the boys, Great Gran, and all our friends at the Chapel of St. Andrew's,

The Viennese Ball was lovely! On Friday night, 85 people attended, mostly adorned in tuxedos. The food and music were fantastic. We had a raffle and gave away 170 donated gifts. The largest was a free trip for Antananarivo/Paris/Vienna and return. A little over $6,000 was raised from ministers, embassy personnel and wealthy Malagasy.

On Sunday we learned that the American Embassy would give $15,000 for a fourth dispensary, the first in the heart of the rainforest to be built in Anosibe An'Ala. A local drug company will donate medicines worth between $2,000 and $3,000 for the first six months.

Enclosed is an article that was in the local paper last Monday. It is a good write up. We did not even know it was going to be in the paper, but when we went through the receiving line at the 4th of July reception at the American Ambassador's house, we were told that Todd's name was all over the paper! After the reception we went out and bought 10 copies of the newspaper. This is what the paper said:

MADAGASCAR MIDI
Monday, July 4ᵗʰ 1994

The inhabitants of Anosibe An'Ala are now relaxed in their mind. Their dispensary will soon be operational and they will just wait for the arrival of the couple of doctors and druggists expected to work there.

This is the result of the contribution of many donors, and especially the man of God, Todd McGregor, initiator of the project. More than 45.000.00 FMG (Approx. $21,000 USD) has been collected lately for the running of this dispensary.

Anosibe An'Ala will not anymore be a rainforest where patients have only to wait for death. A ball can bring a lot especially when generosity shows itself. This was the case on June 3ʳᵈ, during the "Viennese Ball" when the jet-society of Antananarivo was gathered at the D'Adesky couple's residence. The party collected 11.350.000 FMG (approx. 6,000 USD) and this sum was fully entrusted to Todd McGregor.

The Ambassador of the United States is always ready for encouraging and supporting micro-projects of this kind. He has covered the difference between the total cost of the project and the funds collected during this "Viennese Ball." The total of the sum collected is evaluated at more than 45.000.000 FMG.

This sum will be for the pharmaceutical supplies; the six months float for medicines, and the setting up of a nutritional center at the dispensary. The construction of this dispensary, the fourth dealt with by Todd McGregor, began around mid-June of this year and will be finished in the first semester of 1995 in order to bring improvement into the health conditions of approximately 25,000 inhabitants of this region, enclosed in the province of Toamasina.

For information, notice that 27 "generous hands" whose firms, financial institutions, diplomatic representatives, either here in Madagascar or abroad (Germany, Austria), contributed to the realization of this party which took place on June 3, 1994 at Ambatomaro. (Translated from French, into English)

LIII
Todd's 142 KM Hike

9 July 1994

Dear Mom and Dad,

We just finished a baking double batch of chocolate chip cookies and a batch of banana muffins. Corbi has placed them on a plate in the dining room awaiting her daddy's arrival from the rainforest. Todd left for his 142-kilometer hike on Monday at 4:00 p.m. He and his new assistant, Gaby, were to sleep overnight in Moramanga (2-3 hours by taxi-bus) on Monday and then start their trek to the site of the 4th dispensary on Tuesday (early in the morning), walking 3 full days and then spending time in the village with carpenters and other workers. This is a trip, which would have been perfect with a helicopter, but they have none.

Todd will come home exhausted, only to leave on another 3 day jaunt tomorrow in the morning, assuming he arrives home today. This one consists of a short 18-kilometer walk to the village of Ramainandro, where the Bishop will be giving the blessing for the 3rd dispensary. The dispensary opened in May, but the "blessing" was postponed due to the rainy seasons. Now the road should be dry.

Quite a crew is going. Bishop, Mme Elisabeth and two of their children, the Smiths' (British Ambassador and his wife) their nephew, visiting from England, the US AID Head of Finances and two USAID employees. Trish is adventuring with me – leaving Monday morning, travelling five hours by personal car, sleeping in Faratsiho, walking 18 kilometers in the morning. Monday evening we shall be sleeping in the rustic facilities of the old missionaries house. Corbi and Charese are staying with the Martins for 2 days.

Fara's wedding was lovely. Timing does not seem to matter, however. The groom was only four hours late! Todd drove the college land Rover as the wedding car!

I have been playing tennis with Peter Smith (British Ambassador) once a week, on Wednesday afternoons. We have a really fun time together and it is a real stress reliever for him. The first time we played we played for 3,000,000 FMG! At least that was Peter's joke. Before we played (when we were having lunch at their place) he read a letter from Todd requesting 3,000,000 FMG more to finish the dispensary at Ramainandro. After Peter read the letter he said, OK Patsy, this match is worth 3,000,000 FMG!) Thank goodness I won. Our abilities are very close – I won the first 2 times we played and he won last week.

Suzanne (his wife) and I are very good friends. On the 18th of July we are going to walk from Ambatoharanana to Ambohimanga (2 hours). We will have the chauffeur drop us off at one end and pick us up on the other. She wants to invite the US Ambassador's wife, the Swiss Ambassador's wife, and the German Ambassador's wife. She said her Embassy friends need to get out on an adventure.

LIV
Our Third Funeral

14 July 1994

Dear Mom and Dad,

Yesterday we attended the funeral of David, the Bishop's Secretary. David was a friend of ours because we worked closely with him, especially during our first year here when we lived "in town." David died very suddenly of high blood pressure. Last Tuesday he worked, Wednesday he went into the hospital, Friday he was unconscious, and Saturday morning, at 5:30, he died. It seems so strange. We ask ourselves so many questions. Could not the hospitals have done anything for him? Was the equipment not enough? Was their knowledge not enough? Why did this man, probably in his mid-fifties with five children (four in University) die? It is difficult to get a straight answer, perhaps because of the language gap, or perhaps because nobody really knows. All that is said is "it was so sudden."

Yesterday Todd and I attended the funeral. It was a whole day affair. First we went to the house in the morning to offer our condolences and give a small envelope containing a financial gift. Then, the funeral was at 1:30 p.m. followed by the burial out in the country (towards Ambatoharanana.) We finally left the gravesite at 5:40 p.m. making it a very long day. The Bishop looked tired and weary, both physically and emotionally. Please remember to pray for him. They have an important Synod meetings coming up in two weeks time, and I am sure that he is under pressure with work, and now even more so with the death of his secretary.

LV
The Three-Wheel Drive

4 Aug 1994

Greetings from Madagascar!

The SOMA (Sharing Of Ministry Abroad) team are here. The team consists of two couples. Living in the country with no running water does not seem to bother them. They brought our tickets from Australia, our passports from Mauritius, and our agenda for our two weeks in Australia. In just a month we will be traveling around the world, stopping over in Australia and staying with Cliff Parish, John and Jan Wyndam, and Bob Densley. What fun!

Yesterday they went for a drive in town. Todd was driving the Land Rover through heavy traffic when he saw a wheel rolling outside his car window! "Look at that!" He exclaimed! "Somebody has lost their wheel!" Seconds later, the Land Rover collapsed sideways and Todd realized he was driving with only three wheels!

LVI
Australia Was Great

Sunday 4 September, Australia

Dear Mom and Dad, Betsy, Ken and the boys and Great Gran,

Our trip around the world started off with adventure. Corbi threw up several times at the airport in Mauritius, half an hour before take-off. "Mommy, I am not feeling well!" Ugh, not again! It brought back memories of our flight 3 years ago. Then Charese got bitten by a dog, requiring a tetanus shot at a sugar cane factory dispensary.

However, since our arrival in Australia we have had a great time. We went to a sheep farm, rode horses, fed kangaroos, milked cows, held a lamb, and watched the sheep dog bring home the sheep! Truly we are enjoying our stay with Cliff Parish and his wife. We look forward to the rest of the trip. See you soon!

My Album

St. Stephen's Church

Betsy Wenzel,
Patsy's Sister
with Corbi amd
Charese

Todd and a New Church Congregation

*Corbi, 9, and Charese, 8, Take a 20 Km Hike with Christians
Carrying 70 Kg Equipment to Show the "Jesus" Film*

*Dilapidated Buildings Demolished to Build the
New Lay Training Centre*

*The Old Has Gone, The New Has Come: The Lay Training
Centre Begins to Take Shape*

Above: Procession
of the
"Famandiana"
(The Turning of
the Ancestors'
Bones)

Left: God's World:
The Beautiful
Waterfalls of
Madagascar

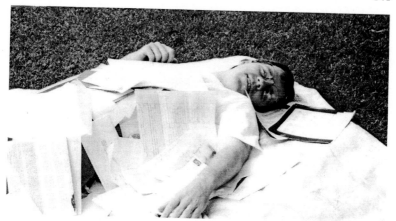

Heavenly Bliss: Todd Swims in a Flood of Letters from Home

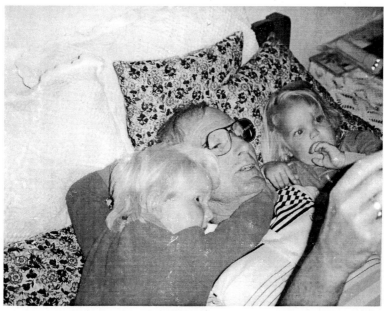

*PopPop Reads a Story to Corbi and Charese During His Visit
to Madagascar in September 1992*

*Above: Patsy and a
Short Term Missioner
Participate in
Building the New Lay
Training Centre*

*Left: Archbishop Remi
and Madame Elizabeth
Rabenirina*

Patsy with Corbi, Charese and the wife of a Malagasy Priest,
Just After the McGregors Arrived in Madagascar

The Kids Reception Committee: Malagasy Children Pay A
Courtesy Call to Patsy, Corbi and Charese

Above: The Newfound Friends: Corbi and Charese Find New Friends As a Delightful Patsy Looks On

Left: The Rt. Revd. Rémi Rabenirina, Bishop of the Anglican Diocese of Antananarivo (Later Enthroned the Archbishop of the Province of the Indian Ocean)

The Bishop Visits the School: 11 Month Old Charese Hangs on to Mom's Arm as Patsy Heeds Bishop Rémi's Words of Wisdom. The School Administrator Stands in Attention on the Left

The Mission House in Ambatoharanana

Left: The McGregor Trio: Corbi, Patsy, and Charese

Below: The Precarious Bridge on the Way to St. Paul's

The Only Road North

Adventure in a Dug-Out Canoe

On Top of the World: Patsy and Dad

*Lunchbreak under a
Charcoal Cart*

Velo and Patsy Design a Tablecloth

*A Dream Come True: The Dedication Service of the
Cathedral Built with the Generous Help from a Parishioner
of St. David's Episcopal Church, Glenview, Illinois*

The Banquet in the Wilderness: Todd Celebrates the Eucharist with the Ravinala Community in the Beautiful Malagasy Countryside

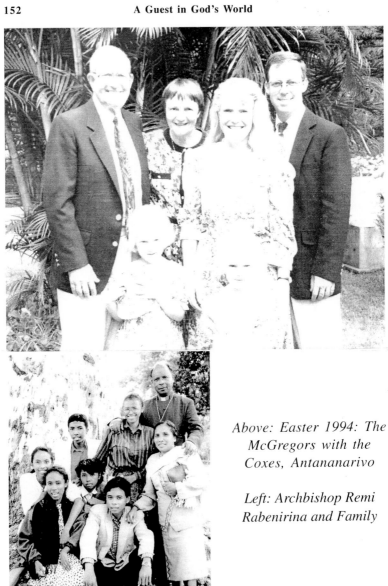

Above: Easter 1994: The McGregors with the Coxes, Antananarivo

Left: Archbishop Remi Rabenirina and Family

*A Royal Priesthood: Todd and Patsy in England When They
Attended The Lambeth Conference in 1998*

*The Evangelism Committee: Todd and Patsy with Archbishop
Remi and Madame Elizabeth Rabenirina, the Senior Clergy,
and Other Prominent Leaders of the Diocese of Antananarivo*

The New Family Member: A Pet Lemur Greets Mom and is Rewarded with a Slice of Apple

Goodbye Dreamland: The McGregors at Their Farwell Party, May 2002

CHAPTER FIVE

To Myself

2 February 1994 Anjohy, Madagascar 8:25 p.m. Cyclone possibility

Here, we are all asleep (well, I am not sleeping!) in the downstairs library cum office. We await a very heavy cyclone predicted to be the worst in the history of Madagascar! The span is estimated at 800 kilometers and the speed between 200 and 300 kilometers per hour! Lord, have mercy upon us! We shall have to see what happens! I am a little nervous because we live so high up this hill. But then I remember God's prediction upon our ministry here in Madagascar and think it certainly cannot be over yet! We are all ready to face this calamity and prayed for the Lord to be with us!

4 February 1994. 7:30 a.m.

Storm never hit. It got abated in Moramanga, lost power, and went north. Thank God for that! But we have been without electricity since 6:00 p.m. yesterday. I pray for protection for all our *"possessions"* in the freezer!

7 February 1994

The after effects of the cyclone are terrible. No gas for three months (the refinery in Tamatave was damaged). There are shortages of everything – flour, sugar, bread, rice, just about everything. The merchants are holding back what they have and then jacking up the price to be really high.

The roads are terrible. Just getting to Ivandry takes me one hour, instead of the usual fifteen minutes! A number of people have lost their homes. It is depressing and discouraging. It is an added difficulty not to have electricity! Cannot do any laundry...take a hot shower...watch a video...work on the computer...or even see during day time, because it is so dark and dreary. The house is very dark with its dark wooden floors and narrow walls. Electricity has been out for four days now and it is especially depressing as it rains all the time. Lord, are you sure I can handle more? You say that you will never give us more than we can handle!

Our car is a BIG frustration too. I truly hope and pray it will be fixed by the time Mom and Dad come! Lord, hear our prayer!

8 February 1994

Oh Lord! Thank you so much for the phone call from Betsy and Ken! It made my day and I was so happy to hear from them. They were concerned about us because they have heard so much about that cyclone. It has been all over the CNN news, with pictures of all the devastation caused. I am so glad they called, it was such an uplifter, and I am sure it was comforting for them too to hear that all is well!

I am so thankful we have moved in town. With the road the way it is, petrol being a problem, and all the rain, it is a true blessing that we are in town! It is fun for Corbi and Charese because they can do fun things too, like attending birthday parties! I am so happy today! The lights work and the toilet flushes! Halleluiah! Now if only the alternator would get fixed!

9 February 1994

Lord, cause me to be an overcomer! Cause me to overcome these situations. These difficult times ... gas, food, sugar, flour ... they are

all in shortages and help me to overcome! Oh, Lord, have mercy upon us! In You I live and move and have my being!
1 March 1994

A Tomato in a Flower Garden
I am a foreigner in a strange and distant land. Will I ever fit in? No...not until I reach my home in heaven. I will always be distant. I will always be far away. I will be a tomato in a flower garden.

18 March 1994. 2:45 p.m.Ambassador's BALL
Dear Lord, you are sooooooo good! You are a miraculous God! This morning Suzie Smith called and told us that she has a friend who wants to do a fund raiser (a Ball) to raise funds for our dispensary. They want to have a very FORMAL ball and invite the richest people living in Madagascar! This will be a very fancy affair and all on God's behalf! May all the glory, laud and honor be unto Him!

They want to meet and talk about this idea this afternoon. So she sent her chauffeur to pick me up and take me all the way to Ambatoharanana to get Todd. It is all so exciting that I am exhausted right now just thinking about it! God is so good.

This is how the conversation went when Suzie called this morning:

Hello, Patsy!

Hi Suzie! How are you?

I am fine, Patsy, and I apologize for being brief. Where is Todd?

Ambatoharanana.

How do we get hold of him?

Well, he went out by Taxi-bus with Corbi. Since our car is broken down, they have to walk 3 miles each way and then they are stopping at another dispensary on the way home. There is no phone, and no way to reach him.

Goodness. I really need to get hold of him immediately. There is a very important meeting at 2:30 p.m. We want to hold a Viennese Ball, in your honor. I need him to speak to the group about your work in Madagascar.

Hmmm. I really do not have a solution on how to get hold of him. I guess we will just have to pray that he is back in time.

Well.... not that your suggestion is not a good one, Patsy, but how about if we send my chauffeur out to get him?

I would consider that an answer to prayer!

It is as if I prophesied this moment. Months ago I had a dream that I became friends with the wives of the Ambassadors of many nations. It is as if God has been preparing me for this day. God is incredibly good and is bringing us blessings upon blessings.

I am so glad that we did not quit when the going was rough. A month ago we were ready to leave this island. The cyclone had left no gas and a shortage of many food items, and the fact that we still did not have a car was enough to force us back home to the States. I mentioned it to Todd. He mentioned it to me. Dad mentioned it in on our February phone call. But No. We knew God wanted us to pass through all the hardships here, instead of taking the easy way out. Now God is giving us a great ball to look forward to!

May all the glory, laud and honor be unto Him!

21 March 1994
I thank you for the arrival of my parents. They have arrived safely
with a load of wonderful treats and lots of good news and fun money.
Our God is a loving God. He has blessed us abundantly. Thank you,
Lord.

Tuesday 22 March 1994, 7:00 a.m.
Good morning, Lord!
You provided a miracle yesterday, a miraculous healing for Charese.
You spared her life! Yesterday she picked up the plug to the
transformer, already plugged into the wall. It sent an electric shock
through her body and caused a severe burn under her chin. It was a
very scary experience, especially with mom and dad here! But it
was also a healing experience because it caused me to immediately
pray over her - with the Holy Spirit's help. I was free to do whatever
I needed to do in order to allow God's healing for my child. Thank
You, Lord Jesus, for your miraculous healing power!

Lord, our vacation is up in your hands. We cannot go to Fort
Dauphin now – no sun – no sand for Charese. So now we are looking
for other things to do. Give us guidance and direction and thank you
for the marvelous way that you work.

> *Be strong and of good courage, do not fear or be in dread of*
> *them; for it is the Lord your God who goes with you; he will*
> *not fail you or forsake you.* (Deut. 3:16)

Monday, 3 April 1994
So much has happened. We went to the doctor's. They said Charese
needs minor surgery and a skin graft. The burn is all the way down
to the muscle. It needs to be taken care of, and therefore we leave for
England on Thursday. Mom and Dad will hang around until their
flight to the USA on Sunday. The four of us will go together and do
"*business*" with USPG at the same time. I think this is a good plan.
God causes all things to work out for the good of those who love

Him, and for those who are called according to his purpose. *"The Lord gives strength to His people; the Lord blesses his people with peace"*. Ps. 29:11

Saturday, 9 April 8:00 p.m. London, England
Arrived yesterday at 7:09 a.m. Flight not bad. Corbi and Charese slept all the way from Nairobi to London. Praise be to The Lord! We had a 12-hour stopover at Nairobi airport. Not as bad as we thought. We watched the sunset from the airport restaurant while the planes rolled in. Quite nice.

Yesterday afternoon we slept (10:00 – 3:00) and then got up to go to the bank. We could get money off the credit card easily, not something we could do in Madagascar! We are staying at a youth hostel – Methodist International House – for $75.00 a night! The cheapest in town (but expensive for us!) with very simple accommodations! But we are safe, warm, secure and together!

God is teaching us to be dependent upon Him and not on other people. I was sort of overwhelmed when the man who picked us up from the airport dropped us off at the hostel and said *"See you on Tuesday!"* I just wanted to cry when he did that! But God is teaching us dependence upon God and not others. Really it has worked out quite well. We met one of the head guys with Tear Fund while travelling on the tube today, when we were going to the doctor's. He was very nice...an Anglican Priest...who spent many years in Mauritius! What a small world! God is incredible!

The doctor was fantastic—so nice and he seems to be very good. I do believe we are in very good hands. Of course we are. We are in God's hands! He gives us the best! Now we need to confirm the insurance...we have sent a FAX and are waiting for a return. *"The Lord will work everything out and I know He will!"*

Monday, 11April 1994
Yesterday we went on a sightseeing tour of London on a double Decker red bus. It was enjoyable (although cold) and we saw many places, including London Bridge, Tower Bridge, St. Paul's Cathedral and Buckingham Palace. Corbi and Charese are going through definite culture shocks, although they do not know how to express it. Sometimes they say *Mommy, I want to go home*, but most of the time they are truly enjoying the experience.

13 April 1994
Our first five days were spent touring London as we awaited medical facilities and a fax from the US. Now we have checked into the hospital and Charese's surgery is scheduled for tomorrow, at 9:00 a.m.

Thursday, 14 April 1994
Surgery was short, simple and easy. The doctor did not have to perform a skin graft as expected, and was able to take out all the dead skin and suture the burn up in a single line. I am so glad we came here! We are mixing business and pleasure. Todd is getting ready to see the Bishop and preparing his sermon for Sunday. I talked to a group of 400 children this morning at a school assembly. Corbi and Charese are never tired of the escalators and elevators with all the buttons to push! The tube (subway) has become our major mode of transport.

Wednesday, 20 April 1994
Tomorrow Charese gets her stitches out. Dennis and Helen Amy (ex-British Ambassador and wife from Madagascar) have invited us to their home for lunch.

Convenience is truly what I enjoy about England. Everything is so easy…the easy life…as far as convenience is concerned.

When we going grocery shopping, it is so easy. There are carts, convenience foods and taxis to transport groceries right to the doorstep. This is different from taking a taxi up the hill and then walking the groceries down the steps and down the hill. Fruits and vegetables are already clean (no need to soak them in bleach for 20 minutes!). Thank you Lord for this very nice break. I truly appreciate it. Clean toilet facilities, soap and towels in the bathrooms…hot running water…drinking water from the tap…fresh celery. Wow!

23 May 1994 Anjohy, Madagascar,
Back to the Malagasy *"stresses"* and life of inconveniences. Todd is off opening the dispensary in Raimanandro. He is quite excited— Dispensary No. 3. He walked 18 kilometers, took a truck for a bit and then an ox-cart to take the medicines. It is a long haul and the process takes a while, but God is good and Todd enjoys it.

Here we have a house filled with guests. I am content here in Madagascar, although I am much more impatient with taxi drivers, saying the price is much too expensive, and people at the market haggling me.

I have decided that Todd and I are never going to live a *"stress-free"* life. Sometimes I jut wish it was a lower level of stress…but rather I need to learn how to endure. Lord, you promised that trials produce perseveranc, perseverance produces character, and character, true godliness. Have your will done in me.

Saturday, 4 June 1994
Last night was an enjoyable evening…it was the Viennese Ball (Ambassador's Ball) at Daphne's house. The food and drinks were delicious and they had a nice orchestra to which we could dance all night! We got home at 2:00 a.m., and the night soared like the wind!

What a way to raise money for a dispensary! That was easy for us, but I am sure very difficult for Daphne to organize! They raised

10,000,000 FMG, and hopefully made some more contacts to help out! I felt like Cinderella at the Prince's ball!

8 July 1994
Todd took a 150 km trek to Anosibe An'Ala to check out the site for the 4ᵗʰ dispensary.

15 July 1994
Todd is gone again, this time to Raimanandro. He did the 14 km hike I did on Monday, and now he is probably waiting for the taxi-bus.

Great opening at the dispensary. Lots of people. What a crowd! To quote British Ambassador Peter Smith, the road to Raimanandro is *"diabolical"*

Todd finally arrived last Saturday at 11:00 p.m. from the rainforest. He walked 71 km and spent 2 nights sleeping on jerry cans in a tractor. He was glad to be home. Home?

10 August 1994 End of 1ˢᵗ 3-year term
"I removed the burden from their shoulders; their hands were set free from the basket. In your distress you called and I rescued you, I answered you out of a thundercloud; I tested you at the waters of Meribah." (Psalm 81:6,7)

Thursday, 1 September 1994
On the airplane to Mauritius! Not only did we make it to the airport (Wilma was 40 minutes late picking us up.) but also we made it through the first half of our 6-year term!

Friday 2 September 1994
Charese got bitten by a dog yesterday and we went to a dispensary. No charge…but a frightful experience for Charese.

Saturday, 3 September. Western Australia
We survived the six and a half hour flight yesterday. No further problems after Corbi threw-up many times at the airport in Mauritius. That episode brought back bad memories of our first flight to Madagascar just over 3 years ago!

Wednesday, 7 September 1994
Cliff and Nola Parrish's home, Williams, Western Australia.
I hear a hymn next door at the church in a funeral service. It is a hymn that I recognize in the Malagasy language. Truly it is a small world – unified by one Holy Spirit.

One Holy Spirit who guides our tongues and our lips. One Holy Spirit who caused Sister Novice Hannah Joy and I to speak in the same tongue. I knew not what the interpretation was but the Lord spoke through Novice Hannah, "*Let God.*" The message was given to the young Malagasy teenager.

One Spirit who gave me a dream eight years ago (or so) and the interpretation three weeks ago. Mary Rose, (from the rainforest) will take up the cross and follow Christ. When my race is finished and when I am weary, Mary Rose will continue the race. God will work through Mary Rose in a powerful way. She is a gifted disciple and God will cause those gifts to grow.

Wednesday, 14 September 1994
I said a prayer for Bishop Remi and Todd, based on Eph. 1:17-23

19 September 1994
Stevie and John's house; Phoenix AZ; Grace Chapel; Prophecy over Todd:
Todd is like a carpenter's tool, the tool used to measure whether or not a surface is level. Todd too is like that tool. People use him as an

example to measure themselves and their relationship with God. Todd is a mighty man, a man of integrity.

We just bought a car in Phoenix. The young salesman thought uncanny that we were REALLY missionaries. He could not believe it! He asked us all kinds of questions when filling out papers. Occupation: missionaries. Employer: God. (That would not pass. So he put EWM) Sure, we are the missionaries, that is our title, our occupation, just like a pilot's a pilot, a lawyer's a lawyer. But we are all PEOPLE REACHING PEOPLE. We could not do it without the body of Christ and each person's support. The hand would not be there if it did not have the wrist, forearm, upper arm and shoulder to support it. We are so thankful to our supporters being part of the body of Christ. We thank them for being PEOPLE REACHING PEOPLE along with us in Madagascar.

Friday, 28 September 1994
We received a great welcome on our *"homecoming"* at Miami Airport. There were banners, posters, signs and everybody from the Chapel of St Andrews was at the airport.

November 2 1994
God is filling me. He is sustaining me. He is providing all my needs. He is a great God. The ECW Board of Directors dropped off a $250.00 check this morning to be used towards a coat and a pair of slacks. Praise be to Thee, O God!

Friday, 2 December 1994 Glenview, IL; Blankenship's home
I am tired of continually travelling...continually *"moving"*...continually doing from house to house. Although I am thankful the Blankenship's are allowing us to live in their home (it has been great to be with them). It is hard. I feel like such a misfit. I have nothing in common with the other women of my age. I am looking for that *"spiritual friend"* to be accountable to.

4 January 1995 Koontz's house
Please forgive me for being content only on *"conditions"*. You say to rejoice always and to give thanks for all things.

I have been finding this difficult lately. Moving from house to house, week-to-week or even month to month is quite draining. Help me to remember, *"Happiness can be felt only if you do not set conditions."*(Author: Rubenstein).

Most people ask for happiness on condition. Lord, please forgive me for accepting life only by condition. May I accept my circumstances and overcome them.

Monday, 27 February 1995
We all live in temporary *"earthly"* dwellings. All our possessions, talents and even our bodies will someday pass away and we will finally get to our true destination – heaven.

In the meantime we all live a temporary life on this earth, a nomadic life, if you please, passing from one destination to another.

Some of us have nicer *"tents"* than others. Some have two-man pup tents; others have pop-up trailers, and finally some have luxurious mobile homes. But it is true that all this will pass away. We all are just travelling through this life – a journey to our final destination – our true Promised Land – HEAVEN!

It has been encouraging to look back at my journal for the previous year's journalizing. Well, encouraging when I read the actual day-to-day stuff and how God works in miraculous ways and puts the puzzle pieces together…but confirming that last year (February 1994 – February 1995) was a difficult year! So difficult I did not even want to write in my journal!

Well, maybe God is uplifting me again. I pray for a renewed desire to write in my journal…it is so important! So much has happened in the last year…

We are living in a new country, still in a far and distant land, and trying to adjust to life in America. We have traveled around the world and seen places that we have only dreamt of before – England, Australia. The life of Charise, one of our children was spared and we count each day of our lives together a blessing. May the Lord continue to give us all strength, peace and love.

28 March 1995
Todd is again in seminary. It looks like it will be for one year. We are moving now…and in another two months…and another two months after that. With young children this is a challenge. As missionaries on furlough, we are dealing with a lot of stress.

Lord, please give me strength to endure. You promise that trials produce perseverance, perseverance, character and character godliness. I do not remember the exact quote. Lord, strengthen me and grant me wisdom and endurance, Thank you I will trust in you.

3 July 1995 Kanuga
The Lord is doing a work in my life. He is breaking down the walls around me and building up the ministry and His gifts within me. I just had a workshop on song writing. The Lord is stirring something within me. I can sense it. Lynn DeShazo (publisher for Integrity music) prayed over me. I sensed an overwhelming presence of the Lord our God.

A lady spoke to me about Madagascar in these words:

*I used to work in a museum in Southern Carolina. There I
learnt the story of how the rice plantations were worked and cultured
here in America. The best seeds always came from Madagascar.*

This story stirred up a parable within me. Madagascar produces
the best seeds. What seeds? The seed of faith that nurtures and causes
the gift to grow. We all have gifts inside us but God causes the
growth. We need to be nurtured and use the seed of faith within us to
bring new fruits, new adventures, to culture new things.

Lord, come upon Todd and I in a powerful way. Cause our
ministry to gain a new vision. Cause us to come to you, as a couple
that desire to serve you together. Break down the walls of fear, which
become a barrier from truly serving you. Lord God, come Holy Spirit.
Cause your seed of faith to be sprouted within us.

8 July 1995 Kanuga
Prophecy over Todd: One of the most impacting happenings was
when Bishop Pytches called four people out of the group of 350, one
of whom was Todd, and the group prophesied over them. The
prophecies or words of knowledge for Todd were very powerful,
confirming the call, which we have known for awhile, bringing
edification and encouragement. People spoke:

Apostleship (the wife of David Pytches)
An inner security to handle that leadership
Peace which follows after you like a train (David Pytches
praying over Todd and said that Todd would be a
peacemaker)
Psalm 23 equated with finances

A day later, when Bishop Pytches was praying over Todd and I
as a couple – he said that God was going to bless Todd with dreams
and revelations, and me with a double sensitivity of discernment!
We thought maybe he got his hands mixed up! It seems as though I

am the prophet and Todd is the one gifted with discernment! Lord, use us in our strengths and our weaknesses!

Now, what does Psalm 23 say for us in regards to finances? Lord, please open my heart, soul and mind, to see your word.

The Lord is my shepherd
(The Lord is my caretaker)

I shall not want
(I shall not be anxious for anything)

He makes me lie down in green pastures
(He will give us the money for beautiful vacations)

He leads me besides quiet waters
(He will pull us away to quiet places)

He restores my soul
(He will give us R & R – so important!)

He guides me in the paths of righteousness
(He will keep us in His Word)

For His name's sake
(To God be the Glory!)

Even though I walk through the valley
of the shadow of death
(Life is not a bed of roses)

I fear no evil
(Nothing can harm me!)

For Thou art with me
(God is continually beside us.)

Thy rod and Thy staff, they comfort me
(He is in control and this brings us peace!)

Thou dost prepare a table before me
in the presence of my enemies
(He has ordained our lives)

Thou hast anointed my head with oil
(He has called us, commissioned us and sent us out.)

My cup overflows
(He will bless us abundantly!)

Surely goodness and loving-kindness will
follow me all the days of my life. And I will
dwell in the house of the Lord forever!
(We are guests in God's world!)

CHAPTER SIX

America Ho!

I

Aunt Betsy, What is a Postman?

It was a lovely fall day in Southeast Florida. The sun was brightly shining and a calm breeze made the northerners jealous of the delightful temperature. Corbi and Charese were in the front yard, playing with my sister's two boys. They were having a delightful time doing the things that were not easy for them to do in Madagascar, like riding bikes with training wheels, running through the sprinkler and playing at the school park on the other side of the neighbor's house. Swings, teeter-totters and merry-go-rounds held extra fascination to the children, as they did not have these luxuries in Madagascar. The best for them was to be able to play with their cousins, who they dearly missed while in Madagascar. When the summer heat became overwhelming, the four cousins would quench their thirst and cool off with popsicles and lemonade.

About 10:00 a.m. I had taken the opportunity to run errands while my dear sister said she would watch the children. She was out gardening, puttering around the house— as my mom would call it. A man, carrying a leather saddlebag over his shoulder, came to her door. He slipped a few letters in the small black metal container by the door that said *"Wenzel"* and left.

In undulating curiosity, Corbi ran over and asked, *Aunt Betsy! Who was that? That was the postman*! Corbi's curiosity continued and the five-year old asked, *what is a postman*?

Corbi's recollection of receiving mail in Madagascar was once a week. David, the college administrator, would bring the few letters that we received via the Bishop's house. David was our "mailman" and the post office truck was a white landrover. Most of the letters came from Mom and Dad, Betsy, and Ken, and faithful friends. Technology was not yet set up for email and those letters came like a nugget of gold to the searching miner.

My parents and sister had great fun showing "new" things to Corbi and Charese. Once my mother came back to the house all excited because she showed her grandchildren how to use the coke machine. Corbi stood in front of the red and white iron machine and said, *what in the world is that*?

Going out at night was also a new adventure. Corbi was not used to streetlights and before going out she would always ask, *where is the flashlight*? I had to explain what a *"Kleenex"* was, and when they discovered all the TV channels and Captain Crunch cereal, I knew they had the morning occupied.

In kindergarten, Corbi was frustrated because she could not draw a zebra. Finally she gave up and asked her teacher if she could draw a lemur instead. McDonalds was also a new discovery, and either Corbi or Charese could usually coax PopPop into taking them out for a meal. Was it the toy or the cheeseburger that held that special attraction?

All the new discoveries were delightful. Watching movies on a large screen while eating buttered popcorn that leaves oil stains on your fingers. Aisles of supermarket products, bubble gum machines, traffic lights and stop signs. And finally, the reassurance that we resembled those around us, *Mom, they are all the same color* (we lived in a predominately white neighborhood), *they all speak the same language and, they all like the same foods that we like!*

My father says, *all people grow up three times. Once themselves, once when they have children and once when they have grandchildren.* Throughout our lives, we all have growth spurts. We grow up a second time when we look through the eyes of a child. Pink cotton candy exudes a flowery aroma. White puffy clouds form new shape. The ocean has a deeper blue and the sand slipping between our toes revives our soul. Donuts have a bigger hole and we always want just one more!

II

Corbi recalls a Visit to the Post Office
The Kids Korner, written by Corbi McGregor, Fall 1999 issue of
People Reaching People

One day while in Florida, I went to the post office with my grandmother and sister. It was very different for me. Even though I am now nine years old, I had never been in an American post office. It was very clean and crowded. The workers at the office had many computers and machines. We bought some stamps for the letters and GG. Charese and I put on the stamps. GG taught us where to place the stamps. I suggested that we put them on the back to help the envelope stay closed (in Madagascar the envelopes do not have glue on them) but GG told us that the postal service required that we put the stamp on the right upper corner. When we finished putting the stamps on the letters, we slid the letters in an oblong slot. And do you know what the lady at the counter gave us? A coloring activity book! What a fun trip going to the post office can be!

III
American Nomads

After eleven years of marriage, it seemed like we were living like
nomads.

Nine months in Rochester, NY
Four months with the Harper's in Arlington Heights, IL
One year with Dee in Deerfield, IL
One year married student housing, Trinity (one bedroom)
One year married student housing, Trinity (two bedroom)
Two months at the St. David's Rectory, Glenview, IL
Three months with Mom and Dad, Deerfield Beach, FL
Six months at St. Andrew's, teaching, Boca Raton, FL
One year in Antananarivo, Madagascar
Three months in Antsirabe, Madagascar
One and a half years in Ambatoharanana, Madagascar
One year in Antananarivo, Madagascar
One year in Chicago - 11 places
One year in Florida - 2 places

IV
One Pole at a Time

During one of our years on furlough, we were visiting Todd's family
in Arizona.

As I took a break from inputting my journals into the computer,
Todd's brother-in-law, John, asked about my book.

How many journals do you have, Patsy?

Twenty years worth!

It seemed overwhelming as I admitted the massive mountain I
was climbing. Writing a book can be a frightening experience to the

everyday wife and mother who simply has the desire to accumulate stories for her family. Someday I wondered if I would really get to my destination. Then he shared a story with me that I hope never to forget.

John was an engineer for the Tucson Fire Department. After a devastating storm, the Fire Department was called to help upright electrical lines, taken down by the storm. People were trapped in their cars. Poles had fallen on top of a pick-up truck. The electricity was out for 3 days.

When John arrived at the scene, he was overwhelmed at the sight. Electrical lines had fallen and were scattered like a box of toothpicks accidentally dropped on the ground. Eventhough many emergency crew personnel were at the scene, the process of uprighting all the poles seemed overwhelming.

A few minutes later, the head of the Electrical Company arrived. John looked at him and sighed,

How are we going to do this? How are we going to upright all these poles?

The experienced director replied,

One pole at a time!

Is not it the same with life? Life is a process. All that is in life is part of that process. Whether it comes to writing a book page-by-page, doing dishes plate-by-plate, or enduring furlough, house-by-house, life is a process. The key is to find joy and patience in the process, while knowing that the end is not our only destination.

V
Blessings

Todd's mother, Patricia Potvin, worked at a Christian bookstore. We stopped in to visit her one day. Jerry, the owner, took Patsy aside and told her to take two boxes, assemble them and give them to Todd and me to fill to the brim with anything we wanted from the store!

There were no limitations on what we could take. Jerry wanted to bless us with whatever we wanted. It was available and free for our taking. Pictures, gifts, CD's, books, tapes, videos, shirts, CD ROM Bible concordances, liturgy, altar covers, anything we wanted from the store!

Jerry's generosity was overwhelming! He wanted to bless us and made everything in his store available to us!

It caused me to think of God's abundant blessings on us, as His children.
He wants us to be joyous, overflowing with happiness. He allows us to come into His Kingdom and ask for whatever we desire. There are no limitations from God.

Yes, we as human beings set our own limitations. We falsely think:

I cannot repay Him. We could not begin to repay Jerry's generosity. He does not really mean what he said (anything from the store?). I do not deserve what he is giving me. How can he afford all this? Fear of what others will think! Do you think others will think I am stealing this from the store?

Lord, help me to overcome my human limitations, which prevent you from doing all you want in my life. Cause me to appreciate your blessings. It is more than I ever could have imagined.

VI
Eagle Christians

In 1996, we went to renewal conference at the Chapel of St Andrews in Kanuga, North Carolina, with my sister Betsy, my mom, and others. Terry Fullham and Lee Buck were the guest speakers. Renewal in our bodies, souls and spirits were what we needed. Terry Fullham spoke on eagles.

Eagles are solitary birds, not flocking birds. The mother builds the nests, not with twigs, but with large branches on the edge of cliffs. Even if the nest is plummeted down a cliff, the eggs will not break as the nest is softened with leaves.

Separate an eagle from its mother and it will never fly.

When it is time, the mother eagle pulls the branches apart and dismantles the nest.

The baby eagle is taken up to the heights in its mother's claws. Then the mother would let go of the baby!

Eagles do not fly by themselves! They float on the air currents around them. Eagles are not afraid of storms; because the winds force them up, up, up. Eagles do not flap their wings; they soar on the air currents around them!

Eagles have no peripheral vision - they can only see ahead!

How truly this analogy describes Christians!

Are we also not like eagles? God reminds us in the Bible:

...How I bore you on eagles' wings
and brought you to myself

(Exodus 19:4)

VII
A Quiet Heart

Every man is in some way my superior,
therefore every man is in some way my teacher.
Abraham Lincoln

To make ends meet while on furlough, I taught at Boca Raton Christian School. It was great fun going back, as Boca Christian was my very first teaching position right out of college. Having many friends still there, it was a pleasure to see them again.

I always learn something when I enter a classroom. It does not seem to make a difference if I am going to be the teacher, a substitute, or like today, a first grade teacher's aide. Classrooms are for learning, both for pupils and teachers, as a middle-aged woman, I taught in the same first grade classroom, where I received my education. After all, learning goes far beyond the A, B, C's and 2 + 2.

It was a Friday morning, just a few minutes before the seven and eight year olds were to break for lunch. Only being into the second week of the new school year, and also being a Friday, the children were getting a bit restless as they had their free time. They could make their own choices on how to use their time, although there were certain rules they knew to follow. When the teacher called them up individually to her desk, they were to recite the weekly Bible verse.

As the noise level grew, the experienced teacher stated in a controlled and quiet voice, *you are not hearing me call your name.*

At the drop of her words, the classroom became quiet, once again, returning to the permissible noise level.

And then I thought, God, the Ultimate Teacher, must say that to us, His students. "*You are not hearing me call your name?*" And sometimes we are just too busy doing our own thing, to hear Him.

My quiet collating turned into prayerful introspection as I continued my classroom experience. "*Lord, please give me a quiet heart*". When you call, please help me to listen to your voice. Help me to hear your soft, still, voice. May I always be ready to obey your instructions in my classroom, called life."

VIII
A Cherished Letter

Many people will walk in and out of your life,
but only true friends will leave footprints in your heart.
Eleanor Roosevelt

A bond is struck between friends who have lived overseas. Perhaps it is the struggles and hardships that bring people close. Perhaps it is the pleasure to speak in a mother tongue. Whatever the case, Todd and I struck up a friendship with the British Ambassador, Peter Smith, and his wife, Suzanne. I cherish the letter she wrote to me on 12 February 1995, during my culture shock back to the USA.

Dearest Patsy,

Life is indeed strange when we are in foreign lands. Each time we go home we find it is a great adjustment. We feel no one understands or in truth is really interested in our life and our experiences. Not for one moment do I think it is all their fault; most of our life and experiences are beyond their imagination. We have talked about this before, Patsy. How can an American really understand the poverty here, know what it is like to have to walk miles on bad roads, and to try and preach to people who "dance with their dead?" That is why at the end of the day Todd will be your very best friend, as he and he alone will be the only one who truly understands you.

I want to tell you that perhaps my biggest adjustment in all the years of moving was when some eight years ago we were posted to Canada. By this time, John and Karen were grown and independent, and this was our first time in many years we had been posted to a civilized country. Day after day Peter would go off to work and I was at home alone waiting for someone to come and see me, or ask me to do something. I felt totally redundant. Canadians, like Americans, are BUSY. They already have their schedules and life-long friends. I was just a visitor, and as you rightly say. They perceive it takes time to make a worthwhile relationship. After two months of quiet despair, I decided that since people do not come to you in civilized countries, you have to make the effort and go to them. It is too long a story to put on paper, but in the end my closest relations were made within the Jewish community in Montreal. I did voluntary work in the Jewish general hospital, and several of the staff there just took Peter and me in like a family. But it took an effort to get started as by nature I have little confidence, whereas you, Patsy, have all the necessary confidence.

IX
Another Letter of Encouragement.

Again I received the following letter from Suzanne:

First of all let me say how thrilled and delighted we were to hear of Todd's acceptance into the Episcopal Seminary. Neither Peter nor I have any doubts at all that Todd will make a wonderful priest. As far as we are concerned he has everything going for him and so very much to offer. I would love to be a member of the church in his Parish. His down-to-earth hard working approach to his faith is an example and an encouragement to us.

You were on many occasions my example. Through all your difficulties and troubles, you were ALWAYS a pleasure to be with. Problems were honestly told, never whined about, difficult situations were overcome with good grace and at times your patience seemed unlimited. If you have chosen, like me, to be a wife in a supporting role, no one would ever consider that an easy decision. At times you would feel swallowed up in your husband's personality; sometimes I have felt only half my real self, but Patsy, it is worth it. If you have a dedicated husband (Todd to the church, and Peter to the Foreign Office), they work best if they have a life partner by their side to help, encourage, and at the end of a long day give them peace and rest. You like me have accepted to follow your husband in his career and for both of us that has been to far away lands. I do not have to tell you, Patsy, that is hard sometimes. How my heart aches for the rest of my family, but the good Lord provides. I love Peter so much I can cope with all my real downtimes. I just am so grateful I HAVE a family to miss. I do know what a lovely old Mum and dad means, and a precious sister who, despite the long separations, remains my best friend. We have a son and a daughter who still want to come home to us and now joy of joy, three wonderful grandsons. It is not difficult to be personable and friendly when one has so many blessings. The other thing I hope you will forgive an "old timer" saying, I have learned over the years we are not expected to always have a smile on our face and be full of joy. God made us with the full range of emotions and sometimes we will get crossed, upset, frustrated, and just darn right mad. I think it is at times like this we turn to God and have our closest moments with Him. I am one proud "lady" as Peter was awarded the honour of Commander of the British Empire (CBE) in the New Year's Honour's List. We are hoping that we will be going to see the Queen at Buckingham Palace on 14 March for her to give Peter his decoration.

CHAPTER SEVEN

Going Back Again

I
Home, Sweet Home!

After a year of furlough, it was time to go back to the red island. The high-rises and ocean breeze of Boca Raton would now evaporate into the highlands of the high plateau. Instead of being at sea level, we would be 4,200 feet in the sky. Green grass would be red dirt.

After struggling without our own car for the first two of three years of our missionary experience, Todd and I decided to buy a used car in the USA and then ship it to Madagascar. The Tax and Customs Department would not tax vehicles, which were in one's possession for over a year. In order to get the car to Madagascar, we needed to bring a container. Filling it was not a problem, but making the choices on what to bring brought many challenges.

One day, Betsy and I were having a poolside chat while watching the children climb on a giant, inflatable whale floating in the pool. Sid and Ginger Waits were dear parishioners from the Chapel of St. Andrews who had offered us housing while on furlough. Not only did the lovely house have a pool, but was also only a few minutes walk from my sister's house. Betsy is my heart-to-heart friend.

I was grasping the idea of what to pack in the container. Just a few days before, a real-estate agent donated a bedroom suite to our family. It was very nice—not exactly like one would win on the $10,000 Pyramid, but close. Considering that most homes in Madagascar do not have closets or storage space, only walls and a roof, the dresser and bureau set was as satisfying as ice-cream to a child on a hot summer day. The furniture set consisted of a headboard, nightstand, and dresser, matched with a large mirror. I visualized this new set in our home…a beautiful, light pine wood that any honeymooner would be thrilled to receive. The Lord was good and was blessing us again.

Or was this a test? It was not the first time that Todd and I did not agree. Someone once told Todd that he was like a carpenter's tool - the tool used to measure whether or not a surface is level. The man said that Todd is like that tool. People use him as an example to measure themselves and their relationship with God.

This was now the case. Todd wanted to fill the container with clothes. He was thinking of the poor people in Madagascar, and I was thinking about looking at myself in the mirror!

True happiness is not based on what a person has, but what a person does not have. Once again I had to learn the pleasures of not having everything I wanted, or even everything that was available to me. Contentment based on material possession is not actually true contentment. Contentment has to be based on God and God alone. Nothing else can produce true contentment.

I once read, *"Contentment is not the satiation of appetites but the taming of appetites."* Like a roaring lion seeking it's prey, my appetites truly needed to be tamed.

II
Stuck in the Mud (Or Was It?)

In Madagascar, for some, shoes are is definitely out of the question.
Even if they were wealthy enough to afford shoes for special
occasions, most Malagasy I knew took them off when going on long
walks!

I remember taking a trek to one of the health clinics. For me, I
would consider it long—18 kilometers or 11 miles—up and down
mountains and across rivers with only logs for bridges. For the
average Malagasy, and certainly for Todd, I am sure it would not
qualify as *"long"*.

I was taking this trek with a friend who was in Madagascar
with her husband and two children. Her husband was working with
USAID and she wanted an *"adventure"*. So we decided to leave the
kids behind and go for a three-day adventure, tying our trip in with
the opening of a dispensary (it takes one day to get there). In order to
get to this dispensary, her chauffeur took us to the village of Faratsiho,
a six-hour drive. There we spent the night at the rectory of the local
Anglican Church.

Our first accommodation was quite a decent home. Malagasy
people truly have the gift of hospitality and go out of their way to
give the guests their best. The host and hostesses gave up their *"master
bedroom"* (no light pine wood vanity, mirror, or closets to speak of)
for Trish and I to share a double bed. After a nice meal of rice and
laoka (the meat or vegetables served with rice) they showed us to
our bedroom. Pink sheets and a stuffed hay mattress! Definitely an
interesting combination to a foreigner's eyes. And for what was that
small bucket by the side of the bed? Our Malagasy hostess must
have sensed our state of wonder, and explained that it was to be used
as a toilet should nature call in the middle of the night. The house
would be locked up and dark (no electricity), and instead of using

the outhouse in the backyard, we were to sit on this small bucket and answer Mother Nature's call. Hum, interesting, I thought to myself.

The next morning, the walking adventure began. After a warm breakfast of watery rice and a few pieces of meat, we set off for our four-hour hike. If we moved quickly enough, we could be there for lunch. I must have looked like a missionary from the 1800's, dressed in my long skirt, white socks, hat and tennis shoes. However, I was really a modern missionary as I was wearing biking shorts underneath.

The Malagasy countryside has stolen my heart every since the plane landed at the Ivato airport, and I set foot on the island. This trip was no exception. Like a pot of gold at the end of a rainbow, God seemed to have placed a reward toward the end of our journey— a beautiful waterfall, descending into a flowing river.

It was difficult to fall asleep that second night, sharing the single bed with my American friend. When they showed us our sleeping quarters, we looked at each other and smiled. We decided to sleep head-to-foot, and keep our socks on so as not to share our feet's *"fragrances"* with our sleeping companions.

All around us were bodies in that room. The opening of this dispensary was an important event, and people had walked from miles around to join in the celebration. Many had come a day earlier and spent the night. Like a basket filled with fish, they were floundering all over the floor. Eight people shared a double mattress. Others were not sleeping on foam or hay. The hard floor was sufficiently comfortable for them.

Asleep at 8:00 pm! It is amazing how dark it is when the sun goes down and there is no electricity for miles! We were up at daybreak, literally at the same time as the chickens. That is a different lifestyle! At 4:00 in the morning the sun peeked over the mountain and began to shine light into that dark wooden house built by missionaries over a hundred years ago.

The celebration itself was quite festive. Eight "*mpihira gasy*" walked in from Farastiho (the village that Trish and I had walked from the day before). They did not seem to tire as easily as us foreigners, as they had plenty of energy for the two hours of dancing and playing of musical instruments. Drums, bamboo shakers, and piccolos were the main instruments playing high notes with a beat of four. Women dancing in bright colors waved their hands like birds, and keeping rhythm to the four beat steps.

Hundreds of people flocked from miles around like a gander of geese flying south for the winter. Celebrities came from the capital, driving six hours on dreadful roads. Bishop Remi came dressed in purple. When the white land Rover carrying the British Ambassador arrived, a loud hurrah was given as a Malagasy welcome. Bougainvillea and bamboo arched the dirt path leading up the new health clinic. "*Tonga Soa*" (Welcome) was written on a small signboard.

The British Ambassador had agreed to support another renovation of the dispensary at Raimanandro, a 110-year old mission house. It needed $8,000 for a new roof of lightweight tin, and for replacement of the beams. Work was to be finished within one month, before the coming of the heavy rains.

After a lovely dedication of the new health clinic, the British Ambassador suggested that we follow in caravan to travel back to the city. His car would go first and that of the Martins second. Todd would spend the night at the dispensary to discuss further businesses with his colleagues. He would then take the walk I had taken the day before.

We had gone only about 45 minutes away from the dispensary when our car got stuck. Immediately we honked the horn, trying to flag down the British Ambassador and signal for assistance. However, with all windows up, air conditioning blowing and music playing,

Peter and Suzie were quite comfortable in the back of their chauffeur-driven 4x4 and did not realize our despair.

Walking to the dispensary did not seem to end the adventure for Trish and I. Now it was necessary to get out and push.

The chauffeur locked the car in 4-wheel drive and Frank, Trish, and I tried with all our might to push. *One, two, three ... P-U-S-H.* We worked hard together, but to no avail. The three of us went into the nearby rice field to collect stones to put under the wheels. Each one of us coming back with one, we placed them under the back tires.

One, two, three ... P-U-S-H

Mud was splashed everywhere like a whale breaching into the ocean.

Trish and I were now covered with what we thought was mud ... until I took a deep breath.

Trish, this is not mud! It is cow manure!

She rolled her eyes and grimaced her now freckled face. I am sure she was having second thoughts about an adventure with the McGregors.

To our delight, a Malagasy man came along.

Speaking the Malagasy language certainly comes in handy at times. This was one of those instances. I asked the man, "*Azafady, omeo fanampiana!*" (Excuse me. Can you assist us?)

"*Andraso kely*" (Wait a bit) and the gentleman went to gather some assistance to help us.

In America it would have been a tow-truck. In Madagascar it was ten men, two cattle, several stones and a long rope.

The men harnessed the cattle, placed the stones under the back wheels, and together yelled, "*Alefa!*" (Go), and pushed with all their might.

An hour after we saw the British Ambassador's car drive away on the horizon, we were back on the road. Smelling like cattle, covered with mud, and tired from the journey, we finally arrived back in Tana five hours later.

I called the British Ambassador to tell him we had arrived safely. Of course they would have been worried.

Hello, Peter. This is Patsy.

Oh, Hello, Patsy. I see you arrived back well. They had not even known we were missing.

III
Letters to Mom and Dad

9 September 1996

Dear Mom and Dad,

Greetings from Madagascar!

Our house is nearly finished to move into, but we have only a few chairs to sit on. We have ordered furniture to be built, but it will not be finished until 2 Dec. The Archbishop was so kind to lend us some chairs and a table for a dining room set.

Cliff Parish and crew come in from Australia in two weeks, so the first item we buy will be beds! It will be nice to have some houseguests and help give a house warming. At this point, we still have no telephone or email and are sending this email from Combest/ Friedman's. We look forward to having a car as we have to walk half a mile for a taxi. Fara came and taught Dania to make pizza, tortilla shells, banana bread, and zucchini bread – some of our major staples! Dania is 18. Her father died a year ago (was poisoned by co-workers!), and she is very shy. I do not learn too much Malagasy from her as she hardly ever speaks! She is a quick learner, and for not knowing where the kitchen was on her first day of work (literally - she is used to doing dishes outside after bringing water from the public tap), she is doing great.

27 October 1996

Dear Mom and Dad,

Our car came with the container. Todd got it "relatively" easy through customs. It was a test of character, though, as the name of the game was: WAIT!!! Wait for this paper and that paper and this person and that signature! Finally, after five days of rigmarole they released our possessions.

Friday afternoon we had a special visitor stop by – Holy (of Eugene, who lived next door to our old house in town.) She was trying to find our house and was getting lost. She prayed "Dear Lord, help Todd or Patsy to pass by the road right now!" Sure enough, Todd came just a few minutes later and she was able to follow Todd in her car. It was such an exciting thing to see her. She was full of joy that God answered her humble prayer, and we had not seen them since coming back to Madagascar! She came to invite us for dinner that evening at Claudine and Guy's. It was a grand reunion.

*Peter Smith, the British Ambassador who just left in January,
was in town on vacation, and called us through the Bishop's house
– since our phone is still not connected. So, we had pizza and invited
him for lunch. Even though he asked to take us out, we wanted to
have a more informal lunch on the verandah, so he would not be
disturbed by people.*

*Corbi and Charese want you to know about their pets. We
have marshmallow, a small white dog, which our worker brought
to us one day. Our tortoise comes from Tulear, and our two Macky
lemurs from Rev Bery and his family, who found them too expensive
to feed after having them in a cage for one year. We also have two
kittens, offspring from our first cat Snickers, who now lives with
Fara.*

9 November 1996

Dear Mom, Dad, Betsy, Ken, Great Gran and the boys,

*We had a wonderful time at the 125th year celebration for St.
Laurent's. It made me to hope that the missionary work that Todd
and I do will still be bearing fruit in 125 years! We sat with Guy
and Claudine, Eugene and Holy, and danced up a storm until 3:30
a.m.! And we were not the last to leave, on the contrary, one of the
first! They gave Todd and I the "best dancer's" award – a lovely
cake – but I think they just wanted to give us something because we
donated quite a few things for the raffle. Then they made us dance
on our own in front of the whole group!*

14 November 1996

Dear Mom and Dad,

We received your exciting email with news of coming for Easter next year. Todd is asking Bishop Remi if he could ordain Todd while you are here, perhaps on the 25th of April (Corbi's birthday, also St. Mark the Evangelists' Day).

We will celebrate Thanksgiving with Bob and Cheryl and a group of thirty-two (12 adults, 20 kids)! As their home is large enough to have a sit down dinner for all the adults, it will be a large family style Thanksgiving. The kids will have fun watching videos and playing.

We decorated our artificial tree from St. David's. There are no other visual reminders that Christmas is coming, so we do this early to get in the spirit of Christmas. Lala, the guard's niece, was in the house playing with Corbi and Charese while we were decorating the tree with the red balls that came from Grandma Rittenhouse. As an infant seeing her reflection in a mirror for the first time, Lala was intrigued by the reflections shinning from the balls. For several minutes, she stared at them. I had forgotten that a 13-year old girl in Madagascar had probably never seen such a thing.

Finally, the electricity has been fixed. For several days, we could not run the computer, watch videos, take a hot shower or bake in the oven at night. What a sight to see the electrical company truck with eight men coming to put a brand new line from our house to the electrical pole! Things do happen in Madagascar—they just take time! Regarding the phone, the answer still is to wait! We put in an application in September. In the meantime, some other missionaries have given us their cell phone. They told us it took over a year for them to get their phone installed.

IV
Training Seminars

Todd spent the last week of September and the first week of October in the rain forest, co-leading two training seminars on basic Christianity. He spent the day lecturing and in small group discussions, while the evening was set aside for singing, preaching and anointing the sick. It was a treat for him to see how God was changing people's lives and reconciling them back to Himself. At one service, they had people coming in off the streets because they heard Todd and his students were praying for people. The people came in, Todd and his students prayed, and they left.

He thought the service was going to end quickly since there were only ten people who came forward for prayer. They were broken up into three or four prayer teams of three each, so Todd thought it a short process. As people kept coming in from outside the service went on for two more hours. He has no idea how many people we prayed for and anointed, except that he was dead tired by the end of the evening.

He said it was a thrill for him to participate in an ordination, baptism, and confirmation services while in the rain forest. *"Words are too shallow for me to explain what was happening inside myself."*

One important phrase that kept coming up time and time again was, *"I want to know more about God and my faith. Can you help me?"* This confirmed to him that God has called him to coordinate and supervise a lay training ministry in the Antananarivo Diocese. This was his major project for the next three years. Working with two committees of this Diocese (SAFIFI: renewal and evangelism and SAHASOA: social development), he gleaned new excitement in his Malagasy endeavors.

V
Christmas

I think Christmas is the most difficult time to be overseas. I know many other Americans feel the same way about being away from friends and family. But we always kept going. One particularly fun night was when Cheryl had eight people over for Bob's 50th birthday party. We all dressed up as old people, quite hysterical to say the least. Cheryl had received a box of OLD clothes donated from her mother's church and the outfits we all had on were fantastic! It was a great way to start the holiday spirit with something out of the ordinary. We laughed the blues away.

Because the American community in Madagascar was so small, we had quite a social schedule for holidays: Big parties, invitations to the American Ambassador's home, and Christmas Caroling. Corbi and Charese sang "*Jingle Bells*" and "*Away in the Manger*" in the Christmas program at our local Malagasy church, and then again at our lovely Candlelight English Service on Christmas Eve.

VI
Pet Lemurs

We had pet lemurs – but not in a cage.

One day we decided to let them out so we could clean their cage. Never again could we catch them, though they were very friendly and ate from our hands. Oh well! It was delightful to watch them leap from banister to banister, until they left their remains all over the front stairs! Daily they tried to sneak in the house, so we had to keep all our doors closed even upstairs, as they are great climbers and had outside access to all parts of the house.

Tic and Tac ate rice and "*laoka*," bananas, and other fruits, and continually feasted on the plants outside our door. They also liked the palm tree in front of the house, and picked the unripe peaches off the tree!

VII
Cyclone Destruction

In February of 1997, two cyclones hit Madagascar. The first one devastated the Southeast. Fortunately this is not a heavily populated area. It struck 50 miles south of Manankara. It was estimated that between 30,000 and 60,000 people were made homeless. Many people were found missing and hundreds were believed dead.

Besides the loss of lives, another major difficulty was that the road was in bad shape to begin with, and with the cyclone, it was virtually impossible to get inland. The only way was by helicopter. The French embassy brought in two freight helicopters to transport food because local crops were destroyed, meaning no food for the next several months. The good thing about the helicopters, it guaranteed safe arrival of the food to its destination. This has been a major problem in the past, a truck leaves Tana with ten tons of rice, by the time it arrives at its destination there is only two tons remaining. Someone steals rice on the way. They care more about themselves than the people who are literally starving to death. They just want to make a profit from the crisis.

Soon after, a second cyclone struck the Northern coast of the island. Nearly one hundred people were killed, but it was a rural area, and most efforts were being focused on the earlier Southern disaster. So this latter one has taken a back seat.

Madagascar is so remote and unheard of that news like this is not covered on CNN news.

IX
Ordination

The 25th of April 1997 was quite a day! The church of St. James and St. Philip's was filled as history was being made. Ordination began at 10:00 a.m. and by 9:00 a.m. people were already gathering in the church. Todd was probably the first non-Malagasy person to be ordained a priest in the Anglican Church of Madagascar.

The bi-lingual service was lovely. Texts used during the service were: Isaiah. 6:1-8, Ephesians 4:7,11-16, and John 10:11-18. Archbishop Remi anchored the procession and priests from throughout the Diocese of Antananarivo joined the festivities. Dad was also robed up and joined the procession, as he was one of Todd's presenters. Several members of the European and American communities, as well as Malagasy friends, were present. The presence of the Chapel of St Andrews was tremendously felt and we appreciated their sacrificial giving to allow Father Steve to be a part of this monumental day.

After the two and one half hour service, there was a gala reception with food, fellowship, and soft drinks.

On Wednesday April 30th Todd celebrated his first Eucharist— in Malagasy! He practiced throughout the night and was relieved when it was over!

My prayer for Todd is the same as for Archbishop Remi. Ephesians. 1:17-19

IX
Ravinala Community Church

A few months after his ordination, Todd and I started an English speaking church. At the request of several expatriate friends, we set up our church in January of 1998 with eight people. Steadily we grew and found that we needed to give our church a name. We decided upon the *Ravinala Community Church.*

The Ravinala tree, also called the Traveler's Palm, is a fan-shaped plant. It is actually not a palm, but a cousin of the banana, and has been given this name because it contains a supply of water in the bract of each leaf stalk. Weary travelers find it a natural oasis and the heart of the palm is of medicinal use. It is the symbol of Madagascar, incorporated into the national seal and the logo of Air Madagascar.

The Ravinala Community church offered living water to travelers on the spiritual road of life.

X
Celebrations

After home schooling for one year, I was truly thankful to be offered the Physical Education (P.E) job at the American School. My salary would be turned over to the school to help offset Corbi and Charese's tuition; but it did not quite cover the cost for two kids!

Duvall has asked Todd to be one of his two witnesses for his wedding to Chantal on November 29th. He also wanted Corbi and Charese to be two of his three flower girls, the other being his sister. Five years later, when they had their first child, they named it Corban, Corbi's name in Hebrew, meaning an offering to God. Todd also has a child named after him, and the guard from the dispensary in Ramainandro and his wife, and Tina and Velo named their son after me!

We attended Samitiana and Holy's one son's reception for his circumcision. This is still a fairly big deal within the Malagasy families. Traditionally it is an honor for the grandfather to eat the foreskin in a banana.

XI
Another Dispensary

It was Todd's pride and joy to travel with the children. On one opportunity, he took Corbi with him for five days into the rain forest to Anosibe An'Ala, location of the fourth dispensary. He traveled by ox-cart and tractor (45 miles or 8-10 hours one way), slept in bamboo huts, took bucket baths and used latrines.

Thanks to Todd's hard work and fundraising (American and British Embassies, as well as churches and individuals in the USA contributed), this rural dispensary was opened in mid-October, 1997. He writes to the supporting churches, friends, and family back home.

Greetings from Madagascar!

Climax of September was the opening of the dispensary in Anosibe An'Ala, the best-constructed dispensary we have. On Saturday we had the opening ceremonies, the American Ambassador, the congressman from that area, a representative from the minister of health, the mayor, the regional president of the county and 400 others came to participate. Patsy, Corbi, Charese, Mary Sherwood and the Ambassador flew in by helicopter on Friday afternoon. It was a big deal not only for our family to fly by helicopter (Patsy's first time), but to be greeted by the whole town (practically 2,000 people). Mary and the Ambassador returned on Saturday while others returned on Sunday. We tried to fly another group, Peter Barlerin and his wife Ines and their three children in on Saturday. They left the airport and could fly to within three minutes of us, but the clouds were too thick, so they could not make it to our ceremony. Ines is the president of the PTO (American School) and helped organize sending clothes to Anosibe An'Ala for distribution to the poor at a minimal price. The proceeds will be used for the sick who come to the dispensary and who cannot afford to buy medicines.

On Sunday 83 people were confirmed by Bishop Remi. In the afternoon Patsy and the children returned to Tana by helicopter, while I stayed on for three more days to lead a conference with Rev. Samitiana. Then we returned on my motorcycle.

Patsy decided to use her tithe from Grand Cox to buy medicines. The dispensary has agreed to put up a plaque in Grand Cox's name.

Next year I hope to open up three more dispensaries.

I have officially been invited to participate in the Lambeth Conference, which meets once every 10 years in Canterbury, England, consisting of all the bishops of the Anglican Communion. I will be an adviser and consultant for Archbishop Remi. Very few "non" bishops are invited to this international gathering. I am thrilled!

XII
Two Days In The Rainforest

20 September 1997, 4:45 p.m. Anosibe An'Ala

The rainforest: Ravinala trees; people wearing straw hats and lamba ho of any colors. Ladies wear colourful dresses. Glad I wore boots; rained and cloudy until 1:00. Ladies wearing bright scarves on their heads; umbrellas – black, green, red, polka dot – carried for rain or the sun. When sun is out it is HOT! Hundreds of people for opening of dispensary; rice and loaka; coke; fanta – even in the rainforest – brought in by tractor. No shoes. Wide toes. Left over cement in the church. Wet paint last night. Plaque honouring Todd, American and British Embassies. Baptism for MANY. Hundreds

walked 30-50 kilometers over mountains and down valleys to be
here. We flew for 35 minutes in a helicopter. Such different lives –
all by the same creator. Such different skins – all by the same creator.
Corbi and Charese playing as if the rainforest children have been
their friends for life; no talking but plenty of communication. Our
children have been around the world Most of these children have
not even set foot in a car.

Sprinkles from baptism water sparkle in sun. Spiders – lots of spiders
– in big webs. Do not bite but many of us are still afraid. Constructed
webs amongst electrical wires. Town generator from 3.00 to 11.00
p.m. At 5'2" I am a head taller than most. Braided hair do; both
sides tied at back. Babies being carried on mother's backs. 50.3
years is average mortality age. Barefoot believers kneeling on dusty
cement floor. Outside, SAHASOA providing clothing for poor –
selling at very low price (10 cents to 50 cents) for donated clothing.
Simple people, simple lives - living day to day. Cement cinder mold
in corner with leftover tin and wood from building dispensary.
Women wearing gold (not real gold) earrings; illiterate; but like to
sing. Women with head coverings. Cowboy jacket, "western style;"
boy is so proud of it. Brushes the hair straight. Dear faces; bright
smiles; old clothes. Does not matter, touch life, deal with hardship
daily. Japp's description: Westerners spend most of their life
preventing problems; Malagasy people spend most of their life
dealing with problems. People calloused by difficulties, like feet
are scarred by hundreds of miles of walking. Sweet smells of
rhododendrons. Strong coffee. Children playing in dirt; and my
dirty (filthy!) girls! Houses that store rice on stilts to keep away
rats. Hundreds in line to receive clothes; telo-miova (3-color flowers,
change). Charese, leave your shoes ON! Red, white and green
Malagasy flag. Radio and post office! Quick, call. Someone saying
to another (they did not realize I spoke Malagasy): "and it is Okayed
by their mom if they play together?" (Meaning my children and the
Malagasy kids). The tractor returning the tables and chairs used
for the opening of the dispensary. People not believing I speak

Malagasy, giving me a test as I walked by "marary, veloma" *(do I know what this means?). Children following Corbi and Charese like the pied piper. Tiny huts with thatched roofs. Peas and carrots brought in by tractor for the reception. Sunset, the day is almost over. A short walk in town to buy a snack for the children. Chicken; charcoal toast, rice, and sardines for breakfast. Levi jeans with the tag still on ($18.00) sold in the Malagasy rainforest. Jackfruits, basketballs for sale! Hoops; homemade swings. Soccer field: landing pad for helicopter. Poinsettia, trumpet plants; handmade, arch made out of branches.*

XII
Reunion Island

Todd won a raffle ticket for a round-trip ticket to Reunion Island! I asked him if he would take me with him, and he did! Five days in the beginning of January 1998 were spent on a tropical island, filled with gorges and canyons. We drove all around the island and stopped at its beautiful waterfalls and overlooks. Renting a car, sightseeing the driving around the island on smooth roads and no pollution! One day we hiked to the volcano – a 10-kilometer plus hike down a steep cliff, over a large lava flow and up a very high peak, more than four hours of walking. We swam in the ocean, in the pond at the bottom of a waterfall, ate McDonalds (twice), and drank tap water without fear!

Time is precious and it slips away like a bar of soap in the bathtub. We can never catch it and hold it in our hands.

XIV
South Africa

Two months later we took a family vacation to South Africa. What a great place to be! Great family time and most specially, Kruger

National Park...five days seeing wildlife. I almost went through the roof when we spotted the first giraffe, then elephants upon elephants, lions, cheetahs, rhinos, snakes, birds of all sorts, antelopes, wildebeests, buffalos, baboons, monkeys, hippos, zebras, warthogs, and many others. Incredible! Highly recommend spot!

We drove down to Cape Town, garden route, cheetah/crocodile farm, ostrich farm, Kango Caves. On his birthday, Todd petted a Cheetah, got kissed by an ostrich and saw his youngest daughter ride an ostrich – quite funny and all on video! Kango caves are spectacular with huge stalagmites and stalactites. But the most incredible part was the *"Adventure Tour"* (not permissible in the States) which took us through VERY tight and difficult spots and up the *"Devils Chimney"* through the *"Mailbox"* (because it was just about the size of a human to slip into), and into the Devils kitchen ... all of us wondered at some point in time if we would really make it through the cracks and crevices.

We saw penguins in Simon's Town, seals in Hauts Bay, Table Mountain and the beautiful ocean. We froze our toes as the girls and I swam in both the Atlantic and Indian Oceans (14 and 18 degrees Centigrade respectively). In Cape Town, we stayed with Lydia's cousin and his wife, a fine couple who gave us their master bedroom in exchange for the floor! Friendly South African hospitality!

Kruger National Park is really incredible. Our original three nights stay turned into five. Our favorite spot was Olifants (Afrikaans for elephant), where we spent two nights. Our *"hut"* at Oliphants (with bathroom, shower, and fridge) was right on the cliff top overlooking the river, and we could watch the hippos, elephants, baboons, monkeys, and hyenas right from our verandah! We barbecued at night – under the Southern hemisphere stars, spotting the Southern Cross amongst other constellations. The key to success, as far as viewing the animals was concerned, is being out by 5:30

a.m. when the gates open. This is the only park that I have been to where the people are caged in and the animals are free!

XV
This Was One Time I Did not Want to look at the Road!

I was fifteen years old then I took Drivers Education in the Wylie E. Groves parking lot in Southfield, Michigan. The student driver's course consisted of white lines, large empty barrels and orange cones around which the novices would manipulate their cars, hoping to clear the obstacles without knocking any down. I do not recall the face of my instructor, but I can still hear his voice, *"Keep your eyes on the road!"*

This is a basic *"rule of the road"*, applicable for most circumstances. However, I can recall a circumstance in Madagascar when it was one time I did not want to look at the road!

Not too long ago, I was driving home after a hot day of teaching physical education at the American school. My mind drifted on the 2-mile drive home, and I anticipated the cold glass of water awaiting me in just a few minutes. However, just a few yards away from my home, the road became a parking lot as cars and trucks were jammed, unable to move inches.

It seems that a local Indian merchant was storing hundreds of barrels of cooking oil, to use as stock if a shortage were to come. In order to get the cooking oil to the place of storage, it was said that forty container trucks needed to drive and park themselves on the small road leading to our house. In the states, the road would be a one-lane road, but in Madagascar it is, of course, a two-lane road.

The container trucks being large, and the road being small, it caused a traffic jam, reminding me of the finger puzzles one has to manipulate in order to get the numbers in order. The 5 has to be moved to put the "*9 in its spot*" and then the "*6*" has to be moved so the "*5*" can be replaced into its original position. This is what would have to happen in order for our car to be driven to our house, just a few yards away from our current location.

But the process of getting there was not so easy. One of the trucks was out of alignment and the cars passing on the road could not get by. After 45 minutes of trying in vain to move the truck up and back, trying to get it closer to the other edge of the side of the road, the driver finally found it impossible, causing those who wanted to get to their houses to come up with another solution other than sleeping in their cars all night. Impatiently, I was thinking all I wanted to do was go home and get a glass of water.

Ingrid, our lovely Dutch neighbor who lived three doors down, summoned over the wall for her husband, Jap. She had already been sitting there thirty minutes before I drove up. This was causing a scene for the entire neighborhood to come and watch! Finally the truckers came up with a solution; the cars could drive over the water drainage ditch sideways as to not get their wheels caught in the ditch, turn a sharp right, with just enough space (inches – or rather centimeters!) between the wall on one side and the container trucks on the other!

Jap, the knight in shining armor who came to help his wife in a jam or rather, his damsel in distress, confidently got in his wife's car and drove the four door just as he needed to – not hitting a thing. The next two cars did the same. Now it was my turn!

But not only was I nervous, my car was much larger than the others. What seemed to be inches between their car and the wall/ truck now became centimeters for our 4-wheel drive! Ugh!

Trying to be helpful, the Malagasy truck drivers were giving me all kinds of instructions. *"Keep close to the wall"*. *"Go this way"*. *"Make a sharp turn here!"* The intensity of the voices did not help my anxiety, and I prayed, *"O, Lord, help!"*

Heavenly help came in the earthly form of our neighbor, Jap, who had driven his wife's car through the funnel point, and when clear, gotten out of the car to help me while his wife drove the few meters home.

Just at the point of my wanting to give up and consent to the idea of getting our guard to sleep in the car through the night, Jap came to my aid. With the leash of his large black dog in one hand, he confidently came in front of my car; gained eye-to-eye contact, and emphatically stated to me, *"Watch me!"*

It reminded me of the times when we are stuck in difficult circumstances that we cannot control and Jesus says, *"Watch me!"*

Jap stood in front of the car and guarded me over the drainage ditch, and through the funnel point. Thanks to his firm direction, I did not knock down the wall on my left, nor hit the truck on my right. I did not look down at the drainage ditch that I was hurdling, nor listen to the voices trying to be helpful. This is one time I decided not to look at the road and instead just watched the hands of my neighbor, as he guided my way and we inched our way past the truck.

My neighbor could see the road, even when I could not. He could see if I was in danger. Although difficult and trying circumstances, trusting him gave me confidence.

All of us have been through difficult circumstances in our lives. I am sure that Jesus has been there to direct and guide us. Have we been willing to trust him to guide us through the journey? After all,

God knows the circumstances. He can see the road, even when we cannot. Have we muted the external voices giving us advice, and are we only looking at the Savior? He is the Way. He is the Truth. He is the Life.

I learned more that day than just how to drive my car across a drainage ditch, and through a very narrow point between a wall and a truck. I learned to listen to the voice of my loving heavenly Father who will guide me through every circumstance. He will not give us anything too difficult for us to endure, but with His heavenly guidance will be with us every inch of the way. When we keep our eyes only on Him, he teaches us to look to him for direction. And just sometimes, he comes to teach us in earthly form, such as a helpful friend who guided his neighbor through a difficult traffic jam.

XVI
Bathroom Prayer

One beautiful Malagasy summer day in January of 2002, I was teaching Physical Education at the American School in Antananarivo. Robin's egg blue sky, a cool breeze and a group of 3rd graders who loved P.E. What could be more satisfying to a teacher!

The 3rd graders were running their laps, winning "*toe tags*," a prize given to them after they ran every 5 miles (yes, some children won over 10 toe tags!). Some students were playing "*horsy*" as they ran in team, "*hitched*" together by a jump rope, expressing themselves as a horse, saying "*wheeee*" as they ran by. It was a few minutes into the class, when I heard a loud crying sound coming from the bathroom.

As the door was locked, the guard ran to get the keys. By the time he returned, I had convinced the six-year-old student to allow me to come through the door. She was hot, sweaty and crying, desperately trying to go to the bathroom.

It will not come out, she screamed. *I try all night, and all day, and it still will not come out! What do I do?*

I began to pray. *Lord, what do I tell this child?*

Pray, I told the desperate first grader. God knows our every need. *Just pray.*

Just a few seconds more and I knew the answer to prayer. Out came a smiling six year old, happy as could be, with a new heart and a new soul, not to mention a relieved stomach.

XVII
My Head was Protected

Due to the unruly traffic in the capital city of over a million people, Todd finds it much more convenient and efficient to travel by motorcycle. As he is a very safe and congenial driver, I have no difficulty approving to this method of transportation and even at times enjoy a ride on the back of his dirt bike.

This time, however, it was the beginning of the rainy season. The afternoon rains were not yet consistent, and we thought that just perhaps we could still get to our destination and back on the motorbike. After all, it was so much quicker on an afternoon and early evening when the traffic would start getting terrible!

We were halfway home and the end was clear. The black clouds were coming and we were going to get wet. The rest of my body became soaked, but my head was protected.

XVIII
Freedom in Christ

The following story was told to Todd McGregor by some of his former students who are now evangelists.

Recently, some of the student evangelists from the school of lay ministry went into the rain forest for an evangelistic mission. On this particular mission trip, the students had walked about 20 miles, carrying supplies such as a projector, generator, speakers and other equipment needed to show the Jesus Film in the open field. Each morning the team visited people in the village, sharing the Good News. In the afternoon, the students would teach the people about Christianity and would typically present a skit and show the Jesus Film.

Their mission work continued throughout the week and they traveled from village to village. On one of the visits, the students met a woman named Soma. The team learned that she believed she was under the influence of an evil spirit, and at one point had tried to kill herself. Some of the team members told her that God could liberate her from her troubles and set her free. One of the students shared with her that he had faced a similar situation and he witnessed how God had set him free. He told Soma that Jesus could do the same for her.

The woman explained to the students that in recent years she had become a witch doctor and had made a vow to serve the devil. Yet she knew the devil had made her life miserable. As she was telling the students about her beliefs, she was over-come and started shaking, pulling her hair, and appeared to be out of control. Her bizarre behavior lasted for almost three hours. Finally, it appeared that the evil spirit had left her and she was calm.

Later that night, however, Soma's husband came to the students, and told them that she was once again under the influence of the evil spirit. The students came and prayed over Soma to relieve her burden. The students stayed late into the night, and in the morning Soma awoke singing songs of praise and praying to the Lord Jesus Christ. The students felt it was important to collect her fetishes and charms so they could be destroyed to rid her life of things that would remind her of the evil that consumed her.

Before the students could gather all the fetishes, Soma's husband came around again, telling the team members that unfortunately, Soma was still under the influence of the evil spirit. Soma was running wildly throughout the village and had taken off into the rain forest. The students pursued Soma into the rainforest in an attempt to help her gain control over the spirit.

Eventually, the students caught up with her, and with reverent prayer, Soma was released once and for all. She gathered all her fetishes; medicines, and clothes used for demonic worship, and decided to burn them in the field. Later that evening there was a grand celebration of worship to the Lord, and a bonfire to burn the fetishes, which once held her in bondage. Nearly all of the people in the village came to faith in Christ after seeing Christ's victory over evil.

The former witchdoctor was finally delivered for the first time in her life. She was liberated and later baptized. She has since joined the lay training program and is studying to become involved in the healing ministry.

CHAPTER EIGHT

High Times

I

The 21-Karat (Carrot) Necklace

Christmas 1984 was the first one Todd and I spent together. We were not yet husband and wife, but knew we were going to be. To fit into my family, he knew he better learn to play tennis when my parents gave him a tennis outfit that first Christmas. He was invited to have Christmas dinner with Mom, Dad, Betsy, Ken and Great Gran.

Before going, we decided to exchange gifts. I cannot remember what I gave him, but I certainly remember what he gave me.

Todd handed me a small rectangular box, secured with a lovely red ribbon. It looked like a box, which might contain a piece of jewelry. My heart began to flutter.

I untied the bow and lifted the top. Several pieces of cut carrot, sewn onto a piece of thread lay on white cotton. *A 21-carrot necklace!* Todd said. *21 pieces of carrots, tied on a string! I made it myself!* Like a kindergarten boy who had made a gift for his mother, he was so proud of his creativity. And I prayed for a sense of humor as he proudly placed it around my neck.

Then he gave me the real gift. A blender! I soon learned not to expect too much romance out of Todd!

II
Wedding Bells

On March 11, 1985, Todd McGregor phoned the Women's Tennis Association office to speak with Peachy Kellmeyer, Director of Operations, and my boss. Since I usually answered the phone, Todd said he was a *"personal friend."* He did not want me to know who was calling. He needed my boss's permission to kidnap me and take me on a *"mission"* around 2:30 that afternoon.

With Peach's consent, Todd snuck in the back door by my desk at 2:30 and gave me three roses: two yellow ones, representing friendship and one red rose, symbolizing love. Like a little girl finding presents Santa Claus had left on Christmas morning, I was flabbergasted and excited.

What are you doing here? I exclaimed.

You have five minutes to put your work away and then we are leaving, Todd said. *Quick, get going.*

I was stunned by his presence, as he never showed up at my work place – one hour away from his! Knowing the workload on a Monday afternoon, the first day after a major tennis tournament, I knew that was impossible. After all, a tournament had just ended yesterday. We had to mail press releases, phone in results, and get ready for another tournament starting that day. Was Peachy going to agree to release me on such a busy day?

Still startled, I stumbled into her office.

Peachy, Todd's here.

I know, Peachy said.

You know about this, Peachy? I questioned.

Have fun, Peachy smiled.

I left the remaining work on my desk as Todd grabbed my hand.

Come on, let us go. Todd, as eager and excited as I was, pulled me out the door.

Stepping out the door, the beauty of the South Florida day overwhelmed me. Not a cloud appeared in the robin's egg sky and the warm sun glistened upon the water in the pond by our office. The grass looked evergreen and the branches of the trees clapped in the soft wind. I took a deep breath to smell the air and the roses in my hands, and to get hold of myself.

As we neared the car, Todd pulled out a blindfold from his back pocket and began to put it around my eyes.

We are going on a mission, he said as he tied the knot. After I staggered into the car, Todd gave me twelve clues to figure out where we were going.

It is like playing hangman, he said. *You guess the letters and I will tell you if you are right.* Finally, I unscrambled the letters and put the puzzle together. We were going on a picnic. Fun thoughts danced through my mind. I love picnics.

After about 10 minutes or so the car stopped. I did not know where we were, but I had a hunch that we were still in the PGA National resort area around our office. PGA National was dotted with many beautiful picnic spots with large trees along quiet roads. Helping me out of the car, Todd's arm steadied me. He took a blanket and a cooler out of the trunk, packed with shrimp cocktail and sandwiches. Scrumptious seafood melted on my tongue as we dreamed about what the future might bring. I felt like I was being swept off my feet like Cinderella. After a relaxing and romantic picnic, Todd told me to put the blindfold on once again so we could resume the journey toward our goal.

Guided by Todd, we walked back to the car. Jokingly, Todd told me to watch out for the tree, I did not believe Todd and walked directly into it. Todd roared with laughter and I felt like a fool!

Back in the car and on the road, Todd gave me clue number two. It took me a few minutes to puzzle-piece the clue together but when I did, I came up with the correct answer, *"Patsy's House."* Our 45-minute trip from PGA National sped by in what seemed like fifteen minutes. We sang and held hands all the way. Approaching our destination, Todd turned the last corner slowly. He told me to take off my blindfold. Eagerly peeking out, I saw an enormous 5' X 25' sign, draped across the front of my two-story townhouse. Spray-painted in bold letters, the message read, "PATSY, WILL YOU MARRY ME?"

Like a child seized with her hand in the cookie jar, I was caught off guard. All my neighbors watched Todd and me. The sign had been a public advertisement since 12:00 noon. People waited for us much like a cat ready to pounce on its prey. Peeking out the window, the two little girls next door saw us drive up.

Running out the door, they screamed in unison, *Patsy, did you see that sign?* Thinking to myself, *how could I miss it?* I asked them what my response to Todd should be. Unanimously, they proclaimed, *YES!*

Caught speechless and too shocked to give an immediate reply, I went inside. True to tradition, Todd knelt on one knee and carefully escorted me to sit on the other. Calmly he whispered, *Patsy, will you marry me*? I gladly responded with a soft-spoken, but eagerly felt, *Yes, Todd, I will marry you.*" Todd shouted, *Yea*, stood straight up with his arms in the air, leaving me, his fiancé, startled on the floor! He was always full of practical jokes.

Romantically speaking, Todd has a gentle side as well, and he showed it that evening. He had prepared steak and broccoli that morning and they were now ready for the oven. I discovered that Todd was a fabulous cook. Candlelight and soft music created the ideal atmosphere.

I had correctly guessed the clues and we had fulfilled our mission, but frankly, at that point our mission had only just begun. Eighteen and one-half years later we are still working toward our goal. What is that? To live a godly life as husband and wife and to serve God daily. As we seek this goal, we laugh, cry, struggle and cheer together, as a family. March 11, 1985 set the stage for a life of happiness and commitment. Happiness because we love God and we love each other, and a commitment to our mission each day of our lives. Is it a mission impossible? Definitely not!

III

Be Ye Glad

On a warm summer night, I pondered what the evening would bring. Only yesterday I had been flying above the clouds from Houston to Chicago, on my first airplane trip. As a bubbly eighth-grader, I eagerly explored every facet of the flight. The stewardess hustled to meet my every need. She fluffed my pillow and brought me a magazine. She wanted to make it a memorable trip and she sure did. Little did we know how memorable.

Since then, my long-time friend from kindergarten days had picked me up at the airport. During the half hour trip to her home we chatted eagerly. The sky had become a charcoal black cape highlighted with glistening stars. As I admired the sky, I wondered what was ahead.

I was a cradle Episcopalian, brought up with a weekly routine of going to church. However, tonight my tradition went out the window in favor of a Christian rock concert. Compared to my traditional upbringing in the still church pews, this event appeared quite radical. I did not know what to expect, but my long-time friend assured me that we would have fun, and perhaps I might learn something. And learn something I did.

We parked the car and I settled into what I hoped would be an enjoyable night. I was comforted as I noticed all the kids around me were my age, my style. The majority of the girls had a *"Dorothy Hamil"* haircut, short straight hair, layered in the back and side. Flocking together like a group of birds flying south for the winter, they feared to be separated from one another. The All-American boys marched in wearing letter sweaters thinking they were macho men. Even in the large gymnasium, where years before I had cheered for the Wildcat basketball team, I felt relaxed. Barbara's boyfriend led us to three cold, aluminum seats in the right front of the auditorium. The frigid seats reminded me of still church pews. Thousands of seats were lined across the floor, and the bleachers were stretched beyond their ability. Hundreds of boys and girls swarmed to fill the building to its capacity. The number of people overwhelmed me, and my heart raced as if I was at the Indianapolis 500.

The band blasted musical stanzas that answered a question I had searched for my whole life: *"What happens when you die?"* My youth group leaders could not give me a response when I questioned them years previously. How could they give me an answer when they did not know themselves? For years I desired to find the life-saving answer. That night I did it. The appropriately named band,

GLAD, joyfully played songs about the Good News of Jesus Christ
and what miraculous work He could do in a person's life. *"What is
the answer,"* I yelled in my heart. I knew the answer was to have
Jesus come into my heart as my Savior and Lord.

One by one, twenty to thirty people walked up to the front of
the auditorium. Music continued as one of the band members told us
how we could ask Jesus to come into our life. Many teenagers were
giving their lives to Christ. Was not this something I wanted to do,
or had I already made this commitment? After all, I did attend church
regularly and I was a good kid. I never smoked, nor drank and
disobeying my parents never entered my mind (well, most of the
time!). On top of all that, I hung around a great group of friends,
and since we all played on the sports teams together, we basically
kept out of trouble. Like an elementary school girl playing dodge
ball at recess, I tried not to be hit. But I could not run from the
Lord's conviction any longer.

Playtime was over. I did not have to ponder the decision another
moment. *"Yes!"* thundered my heart. I did want to give my life to
Christ. Hastily I ran down the aisle and met one of the women at the
front. She took me into a room at the back of the huge auditorium
and gave me a Bible and other Christian literature. Praying a short
prayer, much like that of a small child speaking to her Father for the
first time, I asked Jesus to be number one in my life. As I did, a
peace overwhelmed me and flooded the channels of my warm heart.
At that moment my life changed. I chose Jesus Christ as my savior
and it has given my life purpose ever since.

The two friends with whom I had come gave me a bear hug and
we shared the excitement together. Leaving the auditorium and my
old nature behind, I knew I was beginning a new life. I would not
regret this trip for a moment. It was a memorable experience. Walking
out to the car, I raised my head and once again spotted the twinkling

stars. A new realization had caused me to think. The Creator of the stars had created me. Oh, what a miraculous God He is.

IV
Surprise Invitation

It was a Saturday evening. The girls and I were in Florida, having family dinner with the Wenzel family, over at my parents' house, for a delicious meal. Todd had been invited to escort Archbishop Remi to the Lambeth Conference, held every 10 years. Archbishop Remi had to write several months in advance to the conference organizer for special permission to allow Todd to come and be his *"chaplain"*.

It was a great honor for Todd to go to England for this very special three-week meeting, but it would mean leaving the girls and me in Madagascar alone during the chilly winter days when most of the expatriates go back to their families overseas. My dad knew the possible sadness that might have caused his youngest daughter and granddaughters, so he suggested that instead of he and mom coming to Madagascar to visit during Christmas, that he send the girls and me back to Florida to spend the time with the family while Todd accompanied Archbishop Remi to Canterbury.

The girls and I were comfortably seated around the dinner table, awaiting our three scoops of ice cream for dessert, when an email came on my parents' computer. It was from Todd.

Dear Patsy, Corbi and Charese,
I am having a wonderful time here at the Lambeth Conference. I am sorry you are not able to join me, Patsy, as we have three wonderful invitations coming up in the next few days. The first is a luncheon invitation at the Archbishop of Canterbury's residence, Lambeth Palace. Tony Blair will be the keynote speaker. Secondly, we have an invitation for a river cruise down the Thames and finally,

*an invitation to Buckingham Palace to have tea with the Queen! I
am sorry you will not be here to join me. I will save the invitation
for your scrapbook.*

Humph. I thought to myself. I hastily arose out of my chair and
grabbing the email from my father's hands. *"I want to go to
England!"* I screamed. *"My thoughts exactly"*, suggested my father!"

So, the thought process began. All through the night I pondered
my possibilities. To go to England, or not. Usually, when I make
such a major decision as a trip overseas, I consult my husband. But
not only was Todd overseas, it was also a desire of mine, if I was to
go to England, to surprise him. After all, that coming week would
bring our 13th wedding anniversary. What a better way to celebrate
than flying to England, surprising my husband, and having tea at
Buckingham palace with the Queen!

Before Todd left, he asked my mom to invest some extra money
into a few stocks. Early the next morning, after a fitful night's sleep
wondering what to do, I asked my mother if she had invested that
money. *"Not yet"* she answered. *"Well, I have the investment of a
lifetime. It is called marriage investment. I think I am going to
England to surprise Todd for our 13th wedding anniversary."*

I called around for some inexpensive travel fares and made my
decision. I would go. A quick phone call to England allowed me to
speak with the man with whom Todd was staying. A parish priest,
Colin had been to Madagascar twice and when Charese had her
tragic electrical accident, he and his wife, Jane allowed us to stay
with them for several days. I knew Colin well and knew that he
would keep a secret.

Hi, Colin! This is Patsy.

A Guest in God's World

A few moments delay and his response. *Oh, Hi Patsy. It is nice to hear from you. I am sorry to say that Todd is not here right now.*

Good. My response must have surprised him. *I really want to talk to you without Todd around.*

OK. What is it?

I am coming to England to surprise Todd for our 13th wedding anniversary and go to Buckingham palace with him to have tea with the Queen. Do you think you can arrange to have somebody pick me up at the airport?

I am sure I can arrange for someone from my parish to gather you. When do you arrive?

I gave him the flight schedule and he guaranteed me that someone would be at Heathrow a few days later.

V

Dressing for the Occasion

What fun it was to prepare for my storybook romance and flight to England. I called professional tennis player and Wimbledon champion Wendy Turnbull, who actually was personally decorated by the Queen at Buckingham Palace.

Hi, Wendy. This is Patsy McGregor. I have a question for you.

Sure Patsy, go ahead.

My mom mentioned to me that you have been to Buckingham Palace and have met the Queen. I am going to England to surprise Todd for our 13th wedding anniversary, and we have an invitation to go to Buckingham Palace to have tea with the Queen. Well ... it is us and 1500 other Bishops, Clergy and their wives...but I am excited to go. I was wondering what to wear!

Well, Definitely wear a hat, Wendy responded. *Gloves are not necessary these days,* Wendy continued. *Wear a knee-length dress, not too long, not too short. Be nice, but not too formal. As it is a daytime invitation, a garden tea, it will be rather informal. You might want to wear a jacket, as you can never determine English weather.*

My conversation with Wendy was definitely helpful in deciding on my wardrobe. Now, my next adventure was to borrow a hat.

Sitting next to the phone was the Chapel of St. Andrew's church directory. *Call Cheryl Harman,* my mother suggested. *I bet she can help you with finding a hat.*

I dialed the number.

Hi Cheryl, It is Patsy. I have a sort of strange request to make to you.

Sure, go ahead. Cheryl chuckled. Cheryl is always up for adventure.

Well, I am going to fly to England to surprise Todd for our 13th wedding anniversary. He is escorting Archbishop Remi to England and we have been invited to Buckingham Palace to have tea with the Queen. It is a great invitation, but now I am in a quandary as to what to wear. A friend told me that I really need to wear a hat. I was wondering ... .do you have a hat that I can borrow?

Sure, Cheryl said excitedly as she learned about my upcoming trip. *Why don't you come on over to my house and you can scout*

out my closet. Bring your dress so that we can match it with the hat.

A few days later we were two girls playing dress up. I had so much fun going through her closet. This was going to be a girl's once-in-a-lifetime dream, and Cheryl was going to dress me up. We found a hat and pair of shoes, which matched perfectly.

My eight dollar dress was bought at Costco ... a little too long, so I went to ask Aunt Helen, my godmother, to hem it. Of course, everyone is thrilled to help on an occasion such as this!

Pearls...a nice jacket...a small black purse ... shoes and a hat from Cheryl ... and the remains of the hem used as a sash to put around the hat. My wardrobe was set. Barbie was ready to meet Ken!

VI
A Trip to London

British Airways is truly the royal airlines. As I traveled the night flight from Miami to London, I was treated like a queen. It was my first time of international travel without the children or Todd, and I loved the fact that I had two seats to myself. I was also in the middle of a romantic novel, the setting in England, and the plot interesting enough to keep me up through out the night instead of catnapping to get my beauty sleep. I felt like a girl going to the castle to meet her handsome prince. The only thing was Prince Charming did not know she was coming!

The wheels of the 747 touched British soil and taxied into Heathrow airport. Gathering up my few carry-on belongings (nothing like when I travel with the children!). I placed the second hat Cheryl had lent me on my head. *"Thank you. Come again,"* the flight attendant said as I passed by.

Through the airport and up to customs. It was at the time of mad cow disease, so I had to step in chemicals before passing inspection. Up to the customs desk.

Your reason for coming to England? The British chap scoffed as he stamped my passport. It was still early in the morning and it seemed like he needed another cup of British tea.

To see the Queen! I excited responded.

Ugh. You Americans! the customs officer growled. *You all think you can just come to England, go to Buckingham Palace and see the Queen! Don't you know the chances of that are VERY SLIM?*

Well, how about an invitation that my husband and I have on Tuesday, for a Garden Party at Buckingham Palace."

It was the first time the customs officer looked into my eyes. I seemed to have finally gotten his attention.

With mouth wide open, he exclaimed, *is this because of your missionary work in Madagascar?*

He obviously had read my passport and did silent investigation even though I decided he was half-asleep and in need of another cup of tea.

Yes, it is. My husband and I have been invited to attend the Lambeth Conference. He had decided to go and I was in Florida with my two daughters, staying at my parents' house. Then we got this invitation to visit Buckingham Palace and have tea with the Queen. I just could not pass up this experience, so I am surprising my husband for our 13th wedding anniversary. He does not know I am coming. (The customs officer must have been happy I did not start pulling out pictures of my two daughters, as I was explaining my life story to him.)

Well, have a great time! With a twinkle in his eye, he waved me on.

That story must have been better to wake a person up on a Tuesday morning than any cup of caffeine!

VII
Prince Charming Meets Cinderella

It was not a special dress that I had bought for the occasion. Just one of the missionary's hand-me-downs that I have been so blessed to receive. So, I think it must have been the hat. Yes, it must have been. The hat caused my husband to wonder: *Who is that woman in the garden?*

Colin and Jane had insisted on picking up Todd from the University of Kent campus. This was the location of Lambeth Conference and Todd usually took the local bus to transfer back and forth from where he was staying. Colin and Jane were so nice to accommodate Todd, and even though Lambeth was being held in Canterbury, a distance from their home near Ashford, Todd traveled back and forth daily, many times not getting back to the house until after 11:00 p.m.

But this Saturday was special. They said they wanted to pick Todd up at Lambeth because they wanted to spend more time with their American chum. Todd thought it a strange, but very friendly gesture and tried to convince them that it was not necessary and that he could still take the bus back; but Colin and Jane insisted. In the back of their minds was another plan.

I remember the early Saturday evening well. It was about 5:00 p.m. I had driven in with Colin and Jane, having them drop me off at the University entrance - by a lovely garden, where Cinderella could await her prince Charming.

Todd and Colin were chatting as Colin drove slowly up to the entrance. Todd noticed a woman, picking leaves off the trees and thought to himself: *Who is that woman wearing Patsy's dress?*

It must have been the hat that threw him. You see, I had not only borrowed a hat to wear to Buckingham palace, but I had also borrowed one to wear when I met Todd. So, my fiery hair was not the first thing he saw. It was the hat - and Patsy's' dress.

He tells me that he was just about to mention something to Colin and Jane, but then decided against it. *They would think I was homesick with puppy love!*

Just about the same time, Jane turned his head and asked Todd, *Anybody you know?*

Patsy! What are you doing here? Todd blushed like an eighth-grade boy.

I came to surprise you for our 13th wedding anniversary!

And like a knight in shining armor, Prince Charming swept Cinderella off her feet, driving away, not in a chariot with six-white horses, but a four-door sedan!

VIII

Lunch at Lambeth

A few days later we were riding a bus with some of the 1500 other Bishops and their wives. Several yellow school buses were parked like a line of ants waiting for boarding, which began after breakfast.

After checking through security, Todd and I boarded the bus. We needed the appropriate I.D. and invitations, as security was tight. Tight security before leaving would enable a smoother process when we arrived.

First would be the lunch at Lambeth Palace.

The weather was quite decent for a Florida girl. It was not raining and for that I was thankful. Upon arrival at Lambeth Palace, we went through the receiving line and shook hands with the Archbishop of Canterbury, George Carey, and his wife, Eileen. Then we found our assigned luncheon seating.

At the international table, we sat with two Japanese translators who were impressed when I said, *Have a good appetite* in Japanese before the meal. *Do you speak Japanese?* He asked. *No, my daughters taught me that. That is all I know.*

We heard the helicopter whirl over our heads. Tony Blair was landing.

After lunch he was our keynote speaker.

Then we proceeded to Buckingham Palace.

IX
Meeting Her Majesty

The Queen came out of the left hand door, took a few steps and waved her right, white-gloved hand. She then proceeded to the front of the stairs, greeted the people once again and descended. She shook the Archbishop's hand first, and then Eileen's and proceeded to greet other dignitaries.

If one is at the right place at the right time, there is a possibility of meeting the Queen.   •

Do not try to meet her right away, the guard said. *She will be overwhelmed at first. Go half way through the garden and work your way toward the garden tent. Then there may be a possibility you may meet her back there.*

Todd and I did what was suggested. We poured ourselves some tea, ate a scone and waited for the Queen when we noticed she was coming our way.

Patsy, do you still have that small photo Album of Madagascar? Todd asked.

Yes. I had been hiding it under my jacket.

Put it out so the Archbishop can see it. Perhaps it will get his attention.

I placed it beside my white blazer and the words *"Madagascar"* on the front side of the Album got the Archbishop's attention. He came over and shook our hands.

Are you from Madagascar? George Carey spoke to us.

Not usually being short of words, I stepped right in. *Yes, we have been missionaries there for the past seven years. We were there in 1994 when you and your wife, Eileen, came to Madagascar. We had lunch with you at the British Ambassador's house.*

Just a minute, he said, and he went over to get the Queen.

Bringing her back, he introduced us. *Your Majesty, I would like to introduce you to the Reverend and Mrs. Todd McGregor. They are missionaries in Madagascar.*

Oh my! The Queen exclaimed as we shook her white-gloved hand. *How long have you been there?*

Seven years I said. *We have two daughters, Corbi and Charese, who have lived there most of their lives.*

You must really like it there, the Queen continued.

Yes, we love it. It has really become home for us.

That is marvelous. It was nice meeting you.

Taking the Archbishop's cue to move on to more guests, the Queen proceeded through the crowd.

I almost fell to my knees after meeting such an important person.

A friend once told me, my mum used to say to me often, *"I will know I have raised you well, if you can visit a family and be comfortable sitting on an orange crate with cockroaches all around, and at another time be comfortable having tea with the Queen."*

I think I was raised well.

X
Dining with the Queen's Daughter

A good laugh is sunshine in a house.
William Makepeace Thackeray

A few months later, Princess Anne came to Madagascar. The British Ambassador had a small dinner party, inviting about thirty dignitaries and a few peons like Todd and me. Being a small enough group, the British Ambassador took Princess Anne around to his guests.

Princess Anne, This is the Reverend Todd and Patsy McGregor. They are missionaries working with the Anglican Church here in Madagascar. They met your mother a few months ago at Buckingham Palace.

After introductions, I stepped away and asked the man behind me if he would like to meet Princess Anne. I noticed that he was always following, and I thought he would like to get into the circle.

No, thank you. He said. *I am her bodyguard.*

XI
A Tomato Plant in a Flower Garden?

The banner hung in my parent's bathroom. Glued felt on burlap. It read, BLOOM WHERE YOU ARE PLANTED. Given to them by dear friends, it was no doubt handmade by Marge.

It is amazing to think of the things that stay with you when you move out of your parents care and environment. Seeds have been planted within ones' soul only to spring up and flourish its colors years later.

230   A Guest in God's World

"BLOOM WHERE YOU ARE PLANTED." My mother lived by this verse. Due to my father's job with Scott Paper Company, we moved constantly. My parents were married in Valley Forge, Pennsylvania, after meeting at Ursinus College. My sister, Betsy, was born on April 27th, 1957, three years after my parents walked down the aisle, and then my father was transferred to Denver, Colorado. That was when I came into the picture.

Grandma Cox spent many hours needle pointing a circus scene for my wall. Written on it was my formal name and date of birth! Patricia Conyngham Cox. August 21,1959. I especially liked the fuzzy lion's mane raised higher than the other threads.

We were not in Colorado even a year when we again packed our bags and moved to Arlington Heights, Illinois. It was here that I begin to recall. Our dog Jason…the tornado that took off our neighbors third floor roof….the ice storm…losing power supply for three days….ice skating….walking to kindergarten with my next door neighbor, Barbara Heller, who was *"on and off"* my birthday invitation list every other day. Barbara and I used to fight like cats and dogs. I later learned that our mothers talked to the kindergarten teachers and asked that we not be put in the same classroom as we would argue to the point of extreme contention.

In Arlington Heights, we met the Harpers. They were on the other side of town, but we knew them from church. They had three children, and we loved to go over to their home, help them dig in their garden, and then sit underneath the big pussy willow tree and drink lemonade. I remember the big snow day, too big of a snow to go to school and work (for my dad), but not enough to keep us from making it to the Harper's house to play. Jeff, Peter, Susie, Betsy and I would take turns being pulled on sleds by the Harper's station wagon, our fathers steering the car ever so carefully. Five years after our move to Illinois was another move, this time to Houston, Texas. Looking back, this was probably one way I was being prepared for the mission field. Arlington Heights, Illinois, Houston, Texas, was culture shock! Instead of ice storms, we had *"Go Texan"* days! Students rode horses to school.

Marge gave us the banner just before our move to Houston, and I can vividly still see it hung on my parent's bathroom wall. Even in Madagascar, half-way around the world and twenty five years later, I can still recall the simple banner, BLOOM WHERE YOU ARE PLANTED.

After riding in a worn-out Volkswagen bug, (a taxi) which would not be allowed on most streets, I was walking up our dirt driveway. I cannot remember if the car had broken down or if Todd needed the vehicle, but this seemed to be normal in Madagascar. As I neared the front doors, I noticed a tomato plant growing around our palm tree, in a flower garden. I was about to suggest to our guard-cum-gardener, Pierre, that he replant the tomato plant in the backyard in the small vegetable garden which the girls and I made for a home-schooling project. I reasoned to put the vegetable plants in the vegetable garden - where they all *belonged* together!

But then I thought, *"Why uproot this tomato plant when it is growing and bearing fruit?"* Is it just our culture which says that we have to have all our ducks in a row and that the tomato plants must be with the tomato plants and the flowers in the flower garden? If this tomato plant is growing so well, why not leave it where it is? It can continue to bear fruit, and perhaps if we transplanted it, it would have trouble adapting to its new environment.

And then a thought struck me like a flash of lightening. That is how I feel! Like a tomato plant in the middle of a flower garden! I am so different from the culture around me, red hair, blue eyes, white skin. Everything was a contrast. Do I need to go back to the flower garden (America) to bloom? Do I need to look like all the others to fit in? Would not I be able to bear fruit in Madagascar just like this tomato plant has adapted to its rocky soil next to the palm tree?

I decided to let the tomato plant remain in the flower garden and watch its growth. *Please Lord. Help me to be like this plant. Help me to bloom where you have planted me!* I prayed that I would adapt to my life in Madagascar and bear fruit in surroundings and environments, no matter how different they were than in America.

And then, between the carport and the front steps, I noticed pink periwinkles. Science research books write that this plant, indigenous to Madagascar, has been used as a cure for childhood leukemia, among other diseases. The pink periwinkle worked its way through a crack in the cement and bloomed into a beautiful bush.

A pink periwinkle blooming in a challenging environment so different than a horticulturist would suggest. I wanted to be like the pink periwinkle and the tomato plant. I wanted to bloom where I was planted. And then, like the tomato plant and the periwinkle plant, the following poems grew in my heart.

Fertilizer
The garden of life needs fertilizer to help the plants to grow.
Fertilizer is manure. Manure is not always sweet smelling.
My own will
My own plan
My own program
All get blown into the wind.
Keep my ground fertile, Lord Jesus.
Weed my garden, even when roots go deep and it hurts.
Give me water, even when I want lounge and bask in the sun.
Give me fertilizer, even when I do not want to get dirty.

A Choice

A choice I have to make today
To serve the flesh or go God's way
A new day dawning, a new choice to make
Whom do I serve? What choice do I make?

I can choose to die or I can choose to live
Choose to receive or choose to give
Choose to sulk or choose to sing
Choose to praise God for everything

Choose to obey or go my own way
Choose to encourage and watch what I say
Choose to love God or serve my own flesh
The decision I make may our Lord bless

So now in the morning, I pause and I pray
To listen to God and hear what He ways
To make my decisions on what I will do
For my actions determine my life through and through.

XII
Ask for the Impossible...

It was 2:00 in the morning. I was furiously typing at the computer when my husband got up to go to the bathroom.

What are you doing? It is 2:00 am? His eyes were still shut.

I am writing a letter to Elisabeth Elliot, inviting her to come to Madagascar. I replied.

What? Never. Come back to bed.

I did not let his pessimism sway my thoughts. For my realist husband, the glass is usually half-empty, especially at 2:00 in the morning. Concluding the letter, I signed it, sealed it, placed it in an envelope and went back to bed.

What did it matter? The only thing I could lose was an hour sleep and 27 cents spent on a US stamp. If this was part of the Lord's plan, I wanted to be part of it. All I had to do was ask. Write a letter and put a 27-cent stamp on an envelope. God would do the rest.

At the missionary fellowship the following Sunday, I talked to a friend of mine who was going back to the States.

Do you know who Elisabeth Elliot is? I asked her.

Of course. my friend replied.

I have written a letter to her. Do you think you might listen to her radio program, get her address, and then send this envelope to her?

Delightfully, my friend agreed not only to mailing the letter, but to pray for the possibility as well.

In early 1997, the letter was sent.

Several months later, I received a response. With jubilation, I danced on top of the bed.

XIII
...And it Shall be Given unto You

Letters were sent back and forth for over two years in order to make travel arrangements. Finally, in January 2000 we picked Elisabeth and Lars up at the airport.

Having Elisabeth and Lars in our home for one week was an experience never to be forgotten. After the conference, we traveled with them to the rainforest, stopping at the *'Butterfly Farm'* (no butterflies - but zillions of insects and other creatures!) We watched chameleons eat grasshoppers with their long tongues, felt stick bugs crawl up our arms and saw lemurs lick Todd's neck.

With Elisabeth at the keyboard, we sang hymns around the piano, played games, waited in traffic jams, broke bread, prayed and had morning devotions. Elisabeth was keen with scissors as she cut Corbi's bangs and she told the girls stories of her missionary experiences, keeping us laughing with intermittent jokes. Our time together was beautiful.

God reminded me that His promise remains true. If it is in His will, all we have to do is "ask and it shall be given unto you."

CHAPTER NINE

Be Quiet, My Restless Heart

Why does sometimes my spirit soar?
And other times its low to the floor?
Why is it sometimes I am ready to go?
And other times I am down, depressed and slow?
My faith? Is it staggering?
Or is this the cycle of life?
The ups and downs of dealing with strife?
Lord Jesus, strengthen me, may I honor you
In word, deed and in whatever I do!
Patricia McGregor

I
Enduring Hepatitis

It was only the second period on Monday morning. I was teaching kindergarten PE, one of my favorite classes. Those dear little children who love to play. It is one of their biggest joys of the week; certainly unlike the teenagers I had everyday.

The little cherubs were running around the field when I doubled over in pain. I had not been feeling well for the past few days, but I could not put my finger on what was wrong with my body. I had just told my friend a few minutes before; *I am just not feeling myself.*

Gripping my stomach, I sat down on the grass, unable to move. My teaching aid came over to me, quite concerned, *Patsy, what is it?*

I need to go home, I answered. *I am not feeling well.*

After asking permission from the Director to be excused, I hailed down a taxi, reached home and went straight upstairs to bed. Besides the visit to the doctor's office the next day, (and the times I used the toilet!) I remained there for the next thirty days.

Bed rest is the only recovery for Hepatitis. On the 3rd of January I first started feeling *"strange."* But *"life must go on,"* I figured. After collapsing on the sports field, I realized I was wrong. Sometimes life must just slow down!

Ten days later I went to the doctor, and five days later I was tested positive as having contracted Hepatitis A. I was not surprised. After reading about Hepatitis in the book, *Where There Is No Doctor*, I realized that my stools were indeed white (lack of bile being produced by the liver). I looked in the mirror and my eyes and skin were yellow. I absolutely had NO energy and it was a strain to just get up to go to the bathroom. For two weeks all I did was sleep, too exhausted to even read a magazine. For four weeks I did not put on a pair of shoes or go out the front door.

On February 11, 1999 I wrote the following in my journal:
I have been a "mover and a shaker". *That has been my personality. Daybreak comes and I am ready to hit the road. Good Morning, world! Open the windows, let the sunshine in, let life begin!*

Perhaps God is bringing me into a new season. A season of serenity, calmness, rest, and restoration. No doubt this bout of hepatitis has helped bring about this season. I have not had a choice

*on whether or not to get the sickness. But I do have a choice on how
I live my life now that it has been diagnosed.*

*Being in bed for a month has not been an easy assignment for
me. I have always been a "doer" and a "goer."*

*This morning I read a Cursillo article by the Diocesan Spiritual
Director, the Rev. Christopher Kelly. His first sentence was "One
keynote of our Christian walk is discipline." His last sentence, "Enjoy
your walk." Tears flooded my eyes. The Spirit was communicating
something to me.*

"What is it, Lord?" *Then it hit me.* "Enjoy your walk."

*Enjoy your walk. I have always been a runner and a jogger.
After all, I get my heart pumping and my muscles moving and get
to my destination quickly. Even if I do slow down to a walk, it is a
"power walk."*

*It seems to have been like that in my Christian life as well.
Many times it's a race.*

*But is not life more than reaching our destination? Is not the
meaning of life acknowledged through the process and not the
product?*

*Last week, Friday to be exact, as I remember that moment
well, I sat down for my disciplined "quiet time". Actually, I wanted
to get my quiet time over because I wanted to move on to other
things, such as sending thank you notes to our supporters, and
getting my hair cut.*

*In my "quiet time", I went through the motions. My heart was
not really there. My mind was distracted by other things. Let us get*

this over, I thought. Give me my peace, Lord, so I can move on to PRODUCING.

I was not having my quiet time to be changed by God (although He did change me). I was spending time with God because I wanted the outcome, the product not the process.

In a way my life was becoming much like an assembly line...produce, produce, produce. The faster, the better. The more, the merrier. The bigger, the better.

Lord, thank you for stopping this assembly line of life, even though it be through enduring hepatitis. Thank you for being the inspector who desires quality rather than quantity. Thank You that you do not look at what I have produced today, (for I would have produced nothing!) Rather you look at the process. Thank You for being Holy, Lord, and that you are taking me through the process of holiness. You are an awesome God. Amen.

II
Healthy Living

According to the author of Cultures of Madagascar, there is one hospital bed for every 586 people. Between 1975 and 1984 the government expanded the number of trained health service personnel from 3,900 to 8,200, as part of a policy aimed at putting a health facility within 6 miles (10 km) for every Malagasy family. The economy's poor performance has necessitated cuts in their service, and it is estimated that only 65% of the population has access to local health care. Malnutrition is common, and the population continues to increase in spite of a high infant mortality rate of 95 per 1,000 live births.

Parasitic diseases are hard to control, because the irrigated rice fields and the streams that feed them often provide fertile breeding grounds for disease-carrying pests. Only a third of the populations has access to safe water. Malaria has returned to pose an even greater menace since the decision in 1984 to stop the provision of chloroquine to schoolchildren. The United Nations Children's Fund has since helped to launch an immunization program, but hygiene is often lacking, with beaches and roadsides commonly used as lavatories.

There are about 750 hospitals and health centers in the country, producing on average one hospital bed for every 586 people. Most hospitals are in the towns, with some rural hospitals and clinics run by Christian missions (of which we are part!) There are approximately 1,200 doctors, 100 dentists, 90 pharmacists, and 4.2% of the national budget is spent on medical care.

Many people still trust in traditional medicine, handed down through the generations.

The rainforests are full of medicinal plants used for herbal treatment. Periwinkle plants, indigenous to Madagascar, contains chemicals that have been used to treat diabetes, bleeding problems, coughing, sore throats, eye infections, high blood pressure and childhood leukemia. Another Malagasy plant, the *katrafay*, can be soaked in bath water and used to ease tired muscles. Bark from the *kily* tree soothes measles and rheumatism. The *raraha* plant has anesthetic qualities and is used to ease sore gums and toothache. (Taken from Cultures of Madagascar, pg. 71,72, 73)

III
Robbery

We were only 21 kilometers away from our destination. It had been a fabulous two-week family vacation in Zimbabwe. Coming from

Madagascar, we enjoyed the good roads, clean gas stations, and quick packaged foods we could take with us on our road trip. Renting a car, we traveled all over the country, visiting game parks, viewing the big five, camping at lodges, and meeting people from all over the world. It was a haven of rest for the four of us.

We made one last stop on our way to our missionary fellowship at Nyanga National park, Zimbabwe. Pungwe Falls! According to its description in the guidebook, it is one of the most beautiful waterfalls in Zimbabwe, a sight our family did not want to miss. *Let us take the scenic route*, I suggested to the family.

Fog, as heavy as a pile of weights at an indoor gym covered the road. The small four-door vehicle puffed up the road. There were no other cars around.

Finally, reaching our destination, the four of us got out of the car, rounded the corner, and walked the short distance to the falls. Awestruck at the horsetail falls, Corbi headed back to the car to get the camera.

It was not even a minute longer when our ten-year-old daughter ran back to us, as if a trail of bees were following behind, *Robbers! Robbers!*

At 1:30 p.m. our family was mugged and robbed at knifepoint. There were three men, each carrying knives. With stones and knives, they began to attack Todd.

Terrified, the girls came to me. *Mom, what should we do?*

Pray! This is the cyclone. Pray and Praise. Sing. Cast Satan out. What Satan has caused for destruction, God will cause for good.

My diplomatic husband tried to reason with the three muggers, but they still attacked. Even though we gave them anything they wanted, they still were not satisfied. The man with the injured arm slapped Charese so severely on the left cheek that she bore the mark of the tragedy for three days. The other men were attacking Todd, stoning him and threatening his life.

There was no place to run. In front of us was the line of attackers. Behind us was the 400-foot cliff plunging into the waterfall. When Todd tried to back away, his foot stumbled against a rock, and he fell backward, his feet rising in the air. At that point the men ripped his shoes off his feet.

They forced Charese's shoes off her feet and ripped off my jean shirt, which I was wearing over a T-shirt. They ripped my watch off my wrist. Thank God they did not rape me.

That evening I wrote the following in my journal:
The scene plays over and over in my mind...I feel sick to my stomach and I want to vomit. My mind knows we are safe in the arms of Jesus and we are being interceded for as I write. I thank God that we are at our missions conference where people can (and are!) lifting us up in prayer. Thanks be to God. We have all been affected dramatically by this event. I can only ask God, by His mercy, to heal us as only a loving Father is able.

IV
Stolen Possessions

The devastation was a learning experience for our family. Reading through the journals written after the robbery, I realized that God was going to cause this frightening experience to turn out for good!

Journal entry of 3:00 a.m., June 22nd. (I must have been having a fitful night's sleep!)

Charese mentioned that she thinks that God allowed this to happen so we do not fall into the common temptation of giving material possessions more emphasis than they deserve. A very insightful comment for an eight year old!

In my journal, I listed the things they took.

Todd's Jacket (off his back)
Todd's baseball cap (off his head),
Todd's shoes (off his feet)
My jean shirt (off my back)
Our watches (off our wrists)
Charese's shoes (off her feet)

And from the car, they stole almost everything we owned. Coats, purses, Camera, entire suitcases, and all our money in any foreign currency (USD, Zim dollars and Malagasy Francs), including the kids' souvenir money. What saddens me the most is the video of our elephant ride and all our undeveloped film of our two-week family vacation.

But we have so much to be thankful for! What they gave back!

Airplane tickets, passports, car keys (we were a long distance if forced to walk!), Todd's Franklin planner, Todd's credit cards.

Most importantly, we are thankful that God spared our lives. Besides the hard slap on Charese's neck, and the small and not too bloody cut on Todd's head from one of the thrown rocks, we are not physically hurt. They also did not take my wedding ring! I believe angels blinded the men's eyes from this most priceless possession.

Nor did they touch Corbi physically in any way. For that, we Praise Our Lord Jesus Christ!

A Catholic, as I was crossing myself; an Anglican, I was on my knees; .a Baptist; I was waving my Bible at them (which they threw into the bushes!); a Pentecostal, I was casting out the evil spirits; a Charismatic, I was singing and lifting my hands to the heavens.

V

The Storms of Life

Now that it is several years after the robbery, I am especially thankful for the journal writing I did before and after the event.

On March 23rd 1999, I wrote:

Last night, I had a dream. We were on the front lines of the battle line. The enemy was positioned. I wanted to hide under the concrete bench. Other artillerymen came and sat down beside me, assuring they were going to fight for me. We could see the enemy, but we were ready to fight.

The army left their defensive position and decided to take the offense. Attack was the word of command from the General.

I awoke knowing I had to fight the enemy with an offensive weapon. The sword of the Spirit, the Word of God.

Last night we went to the fellowship the first time in eight weeks. I asked for prayer for our family. It seems, as Todd describes it, that there has been a "dark cloud" over our heads for the past several months. Satan is angry as our ministry continues to grow. God is being glorified. The enemy wants to defeat and discourage us, but God is in control. He is the General in command of the war.

He tells us to fight offensively, with the sword of the Spirit, the Word of God.

And again on Wednesday, May 3rd, seven weeks before the robbery, God prepared me through another dream. At 6:15 a.m., I recorded this in my journal:

There is a severe cyclone coming - one of the worst in history. There is no doubt of its arrival. It is coming our way. There will be no diversion. Its path is set.

But our family is on the rock. If we were on the sandy beaches, it could be devastating. By standing firm on the rock, we will be fine.

The few seminars I have attended on dream interpretation, storms are said to be a symbol of spiritual warfare. With the dark cloud that was hanging over our heads, God seemed to be preparing me for something. I mentioned the dream to the family at our morning devotions at breakfast the following morning. I believed our whole family must be ready if we were to go through some sort of "storm" in life.

Girls, I had this dream last night...

And from that moment on, our family was prepared.

When I had troubles with a director at school, we thought it might be the cyclone. A few weeks later, when I had my first car accident, I thought it was the cyclone. And again, when Todd had a motorcycle accident, we thought it was the cyclone. Little did we know they were just *'feeder bands'* - small storms that come before the devastating winds of destruction. One, who studies storms, would know that the worst of the storm is always after the eye. Bear down the hatch. Prepare the sails. Stand strong.

On June 21ˢᵗ the cyclone struck.

VI
Stronger because of the Storm

The same night I dreamt about the devastating cyclone, I had a second dream, one about the healing venom of snakes. Once a victim has been bitten by a snake, the healing comes from the extract of the venom (in certain degrees) from the same snake. At that time, I was not sure of the exact meaning of the snake venom's dream, but to me, it meant healing.

The day after our incident, John Gay, a DFMS veteran missionary from Lesotho, suggested a thought-provoking question. *"What in that event (robbery) could have healed something in your life?"*

At first I did not have a direct answer, but after a short time of prayer, I said, *the fear of fear!*

Fear is so subtle that it is almost too difficult to describe - fear of failure, fear of what other people think, the fear of what might happen. Many times we blame our fears on others.

I continued my journal writing:
Yesterday Satan caused the robbers to come to us for destruction, to kill and to destroy. However, his plan was thwarted by the grace of God, and today I stand more firmly in my faith than ever before. What Satan had caused for destruction, God has caused for good.

The healing power of the snake venom: Snake venom is used for healing through vaccines. In the same way, the power of Christ through His death on the cross is in the healing power of the blood of Christ. What Satan caused for destruction, God caused for good. He will have no fear of bad news; his heart is steadfast, trusting in the Lord. (Psalm. 112:7)

I was learning the truth of Augustine's statement: *"Trials come to prove and improve us." "More spiritual progress is made through failure and tears than success and laughter."* (Alistair Beg, Made for His Pleasure) We tend to run away from the things that make us. My impression of being on the battlegrounds was not a pretty picture...bombs...fighting...strife...teargas...people dying.

Had the enemy thwarted my vision of *"spiritual battle"* so much that I was not even courageous enough to participate? Is part of Satan's crafty deception to give me such a warped picture that I want to hide under the concrete bench, only desiring to participate in times of celebration and fellowship of Christianity?

God was calling me to be a *"General"* in the battles of life, not a faint-hearted soldier hiding in the trenches. I was learning through this experience.

I remembered Elisabeth Elliot's words at the *"Keep A Quiet Heart Seminar"* just a few months before. *"He leads us THROUGH the valley."*

VII
The Healing Process

Friday, 23 June, 7:15 a.m.
Corbi woke up with the following dream: *The robbers took our clothes, put them into square pieces, sewed them together and used the blanket to keep warm throughout the winter.*

Corbi had a second dream; *I found some money (USD).* Short, simple and to the point. She understood the interpretation. *Mom, I know God will provide for all our needs.* Our God is an awesome God. He is working in the heart of my ten-year old child.

As recorded in my journal, I quote; *our family is going through an incredible healing process. I have been changed through this experience. Corbi has been given dreams - dreams to encourage and uplift. Dreams bringing healing.*

Charese has been given wisdom and insight into the Scriptures. Last night she wanted me to read Luke 23 to her, the Scriptures about Christ's crucifixion.

We began with verse 26. *And when they led Him away, they laid hold of one Simon of Cyrene, coming in from the country, and placed on him the cross to carry behind Jesus.* We continued through verse 31. But Charese knew the story and continued to tell me that she was reminded of the robbers, that she wants them to be like the robber on the cross next to Jesus who knew Him and accepted Him at death.

VIII
Missionary Weapons

I have taken great encouragement from the following thoughts of Oswald Chambers:

Worshipping in everyday occasions.

We presume that we would be ready for battle if confronted with a great crisis, but it is not the crisis that builds something within us. It simply reveals what we are made of already. Do you find yourself saying, "If God calls me to battle, of course I will rise to the occasion?" Yet you won't rise to the occasion unless you have done so on God's training ground. If you are not doing the task that is closest to you now, which God has engineered into your life, when the crisis comes, instead of being fit for battle, you will be revealed as being unfit. Crisis always reveal a person's true character.

A private relationship of worshipping God is the greatest essential element of spiritual fitness. The time will come, as Nathaniel experienced in John 1:48, that a private "fig tree" life will no longer be possible. Everything will be out in the open, and you will find yourself to be of no value where you have not been worshiping in everyday occasions in your own home. If your worship is right in your private relationship with God, then when He sets you free, you will be ready. It is in the unseen life, which only God saw, that you have become perfectly fit. And when the strain of the crisis comes, you can be relied upon by God.

God's training ground, where the missionary weapons are found, is the hidden, personal, worshiping life of the saint.

My sister sent me the following poem which I have held close to my heart ever since,

In the happy moments praise Him.
In the difficult moments trust him.
In the busy moments thank Him.
In the quiet moments worship Him.
For in all our moments He is there,
In goodness...in kindness...
In Love.

IX
Be Thankful

Matthew Henry, a well-known Bible commentator, made the following entry in his diary the evening after he was robbed. I wanted my attitude to mirror his.

Let me be thankful .

First, because I was never robbed before

Second, because although they took my wallet they did not take my life

Third, because although they took my all, it was not much

And fourth, because it was I who was robbed, not I who robbed.

X
Ankaranana

Vacations in Madagascar are always full of adventure. With the visit of my 13-year-old nephew, we wanted to make it especially exciting. Being Brian's first time out of North America, he had so many new things to discover. Not having yet been up to the Northern part of Madagascar ourselves, we wanted to experience the incredible National Park of Ankaranana.

Ankaranana is a small limestone massif penetrated by numerous caves and canyons. Some of the largest caves have collapsed, forming isolated pockets of river-fed forest with their own perfectly protected flora and fauna. The caves and their rivers are also home to crocodiles, some reportedly six meters long. The reserve is known for its many lemur species, including Crowned and Sanford's Brown, but it is marvelous for birds, reptiles and insects as well. Indeed, the 'Wow!' factor is as high here as anywhere I have visited.

The best *tsingy* (limestone pinnacle) is about two hours away, over very rugged terrain, just beyond the beautiful crater lake, Lac Vert. This is a very hot, all-day trip and is absolutely magnificent. Boardwalks have been constructed to allow safe passage over the *tsingy*, protecting the fragile rock while you admire the strange succulents such as *Pachypodium, which* seem to grow right out of the limestone. Lac Vert is as green as its name, and if you are crazy enough you can hike down a steep, slippery slope to the water's edge.

On Sunday, July 9th, our family was crazy enough to take this trip. Three generations were hiking. PopPop, the oldest at 70, and Charese, the youngest at 10. Also along for the adventure were Mom, Brian, Corbi, Dan Zimmer, and myself.

Todd was not able to go, but was going to fly and meet us on the tropical island of Nosy Be.

To say the road was poor is an understatement. The first 75 km took 1-½ hours. The final 25 km took three hours.

Dad's idea of camping is the local Holiday Inn.

By flashlight I wrote the following in the early morning hours after our first day of hiking.

It is a lovely early morning in the dark forest of Ankaranana. We had an incredible day – a long and very difficult walk for hours. GG and PopPop did great. I know it was a stress for them. Charese also. She is about the youngest child who has ever gone through all 3 canyons. Theo, our guide said we could do it...and we did but I did not know it would have been so difficult. Three and a half hours of the journey was cave and complete darkness. It was incredible.

Today is another day and we have another whole other day ahead of us. Fourteen km – much of it through stones and rocks again. This is an adventure trip – not a cruise through the forest. As Dan Zimmer put it (when I asked him if Kim would have liked it.

"She would have crawled up in a fetal position and stopped two kilometers ago!"

By the following day, Friday, 14 July 2000, the gang was tired. although GG and PopPop had done quite well on the trip for their 70 years of age. Corbi and Charese also did excellent! No complaining from Charese – a true gem all the way!

Wednesday we decided to split into two groups. After the 1st section of 7 km – GG and PopPop and Brian decided to go straight back. Dan (who's been great!) Corbi and Charese and I went with Theo and a new guide, and were given a very adventurous hike (including a pee stop in a hornets nest!), with many spiritual lessons along the way. Theo and I talked spiritual lessons and word pictures of God through nature. Like when I got into the hornets nest. I let the last guide pass (privacy to go the bathroom), and I had gotten off the path Theo had shown us. That is when I got into trouble. As I pulled down my shorts and squatted, I suddenly heard a nest full of hornets buzzing all around me! I was desperate! There was nothing to do but run away with my shorts still down! (That is what I call a full moon!).

Secondly, we looked at the way the "*elephant trees*", indigenous to Madagascar, grew in the midst of difficult circumstances of the tsingy's and limestone pinnacles. It reminded me of my personal theme, "*Bloom where you are planted.*" I told him my story about the tomato plant in a flower garden.

Most of all Theo showed me that with a knowledgeable guide, who knows the path (he is been working 13 years as a National Guide in Ankaranana) I can do much more than I ever dreamed or imagined.

Theo took us slowly through canyons I never knew possible to climb. He did not give our group more than we could handle, but challenged us to do more than we ever thought we could. He knew the path and the cave, and showed us where to put our footing so we would not slip and fall.

God, our spiritual Guide, challenges us to do more than we could imagine but never gives us more than we can handle. He knows the way and shows us, with His light, where to put our feet so we do not fall.

He is a teacher and wants us to gain confidence in what He has taught us so that we know we can do it by ourselves. On the way back, after the most difficult part of the path, and after we had already taken that path once, Theo challenged the new student guide and the children to guide the way.

Theo took us new and adventurous places. We were the first ones down to the green lake that year. Jean Jacques Cousteau, from the National Geographic Society, had flown in by helicopter to this exact spot, and discovered the blindfish just a few years ago! Theo cleared the path and we took the very steep climb! Charese was the youngest ever to reach the bottom of the canyon. Think of the self-confidence and the determination it caused the children to build! Truly, what an incredible and God-given experience.

I recall a passage from a book: "*Perhaps we should all live as if we are dying*." (At Home in Mitford, pg. 122). So many people wish they would do things like this…and we have actually done them! We let all inhibitions go – fear, anxiety of the unknown – and took our chance. I decided that if I were to die, I would like to die happy and adventurous, not always wishing I did something that I did not have the courage to do.

Finally, we arrived at Dad's idea of a hotel. Ankify was a beautiful beach with a good hotel, and this became the perfect place to break our journey. Our hotel was called *LeBaobab* (named after the large Baobab tree next to the hotel). Nestled between rocky cliffs and a beach that overlooks the bay and *Nosy* (which means island) *Komba*, it had very pleasant bungalows with separate bathrooms, hot water, table fans and mosquito nets.

After a sound night's sleep, we took a small boat to Nosy Be. Five hours later, we had an unexpected event. During a walk on the beach, we walked over to a portion of the island, which was coral. Our adventures were not over. After a slip and fall by Dan, we took a trip to the doctor's at the hospital and he braved six stitches in his leg without anesthesia. He was brave. The hospital walls were splashed with dried blood. I saw them take out a sterile suture and scissors and was thankful.

Holding Dan's hand, we prayed. My heart yielded to his. To see a twelve-year old boy in such pain. It must have crushed the mind of God to give up His only son.

CHAPTER TEN

Goodbye, Dreamland!

I

How do you Live your Dash

We were in Madagasçar from August 1991 to May 2002, but how did we live our "*dash*"? It is not the date we arrived, nor the date of our departure, but how did we live the days in between?

In life it is not the date of birth or the date of death on our tombstone that is important. But rather – How do we live our dash?

I read of a man who stood to speak
At the funeral of a friend.
He referred to the dates on her tombstone
From the beginning...to the end.
He noted that first came her date of birth
And spoke the following date with tears,
But he said what mattered most of all
Was the dash between those years.

For that dash represents all the time
That she spent alive on earth...
And now only those who loved her
Know what that little line is worth.
For it matters not, how much we own,
The cars...the house...the cash,

What matters is how we live and love
And how we spend our dash.

So think about this long and hard...
Are there things you would like to change?
For you never know how much time is left,
    That can still be rearranged.
If we could just slow down enough
To consider what is true and real,
    And always try to understand
    The way other people feel.

    And be less quick to anger,
    And show appreciation more
    And love the people in our lives
    Like we have never loved before.
    If we treat each other with respect,
    And more often wear a smile...
Remembering that this special dash
    Might only last a little while.

So, when your eulogy's being read
With your life's actions to rehash...
Would you be proud of the things they say
    About how you spent your dash?

                                        Author Unknown

II
My Dream

Monday 21 August 2001
Middle of the night, Tamatave, MADAGASCAR.

Jane Butterfield, Titus Pressler, Todd and myself are together with other missionaries. It is reunion time. I am not sure where we are, but it is someone else's country.

After getting pizza, we drive up to the hotel. The girls are not with us. As we drive up, we notice a detour. In the hotel parking lot the military police demand that we board another bus. Where are we going? I struggle. I do not even have my purse, or any forms of identity, because we I had just gone to get pizza with my husband! If they find out I have boarded the bus without identity, they can arrest and imprison me.

Quickly I leave the group for just a few minutes to go to the first floor and pick up my purse in the hotel room. The military officer turns his head and pretends not to notice that I have left the group.

Nathalie is holding the elevator button open for me. Arrow up! "Go quickly, girlfriend", *she says to me. Will they notice I am gone? Thank God the first floor is not far. I grab my purse. Corbi's* "huggy bear" *is there. Do I grab that too and risk them noticing that I have extra baggage? Leave the black duffel. Grab your purse. Run to the elevator... Quickly...quickly...quickly...*

III

Charese's Dream

While Todd was out in the rainforest, I had the urge to pack. As a squirrel storing nuts for the winter, I was getting prepared. As I did not want to startle the kids, I would pack during the midnight hours. I wanted to keep life as normal as possible. Packing a suitcase might cause the girls concern. However, when picture frames started coming off the walls, I knew I had to tell them.

Breakfast on the balcony was one of our pleasures in Madagascar. During our breakfast, we would pray and have morning devotions. I found it a good time to tell them.

Girls, mom had a dream. (Oh no, not another one, they probably thought. They remembered the one about the cyclone.)

I am not sure if it means anything or not. Perhaps it does not. But if God is speaking to us, or preparing us for something, I want to be ready.
What was your dream, mom?

I explained the dream I had over a month earlier.

That makes so much sense, mom! Said Charese.

It does? I questioned.

Yes! Do you remember the dream I had about six months ago? The one about the soldier running after us? Dad and Corbi became separated from us. You and I were together. The men were running after us, shouting, "No redheads allowed in the city!"

Time did not allow much discussion that morning, for our ride was coming to take us to school. But time went on, and the girls and I were mentally prepared if something was going to happen.

Todd was in the rainforest on a two-week trek. There was no way to communicate with him. No email, no phone. I wanted to make sure I tied up all my loose ends if we were to leave Madagascar sooner than we thought. After all, we had expected to be in Madagascar for another several years. We had become *"tamana"* (at home) and moving was not on our agenda.

But the still, quiet voice continued to prompt. In late September, I called Archbishop Remi.

Hello, Archbishop Remi. This is Patsy. How are you today? After a few brief formalities, I continued the conversation.

I just wanted to call and say Thank You for being our leader here in Madagascar over the past several years. I do not know what God is doing in our lives. Perhaps we are going to be leaving Madagascar sooner than expected. But whatever the case, I just wanted to say thank you. Your leadership qualities have been an inspiration to follow.

Tears trickled down my cheeks and I choked out one last sentence.

The past ten years in Madagascar have been the best years of my life.

Speechless, Archbishop Remi did not say much on the phone. But when he saw Todd a few days later, it was the first thing on his mind.

Archbishop Remi was flying out by the helicopter that was to pick up Todd. Before they even said *"Manahoana Tompoko!"* Archbishop Remi broke the news to Todd.

Todd, you need to speak to your wife! She is leaving Madagascar!

Todd sort of chuckled and wondered what his wife was now up to.

No, I am serious! Archbishop Remi said. *She even called me on the phone to say goodbye! She has packed her bags and is leaving!*

Todd arrived home and found pictures off the wall, and a packed suitcase upstairs.

Patsy, what are you doing? Archbishop Remi says you are leaving Madagascar!

Well, I am not really leaving - yet. I am just preparing the family in case we need to leave sooner than expected. If we have to go, then I am ready. If we do not, it's OK. Then I am already packed for the next furlough.

IV
Faith has Wheels on!

*Faith means believing in advance
what will only make sense in reverse.*

I had not told many people that I had packed my suitcase, but slowly it began to trickle out amongst the expatriate community. In a friendly sort of way, I began to be the laughing stock of the American School. One of persons laughing the hardest was my husband.

Ever since the September 11th terrorist attack, the situation had been different for Americans living overseas. Times were tense in Madagascar and all over the world. The Malagasy government became very outspoken about the terrorist attacks and negative things were said against Americans. Conversations revolved around the political situation. The Embassy suggested we get our passports, papers, and a small carry-on suitcase in order.

Todd and I had a deal. If nothing happened by January, I would unpack our suitcases. For me, my suitcase was my symbol of faith.

I was glad I had my journal. I could write whatever I wanted and the paper would not laugh back. Empty white pages became my best friends.

Thank God for friends. On 25 September 2001 Paul and Mary came over for dinner and to help in packing. Paul packed as Mary and I gathered wedding albums, scrapbooks, Malagasy souvenirs and baby memorabilia. Amazing what one stores after ten years! My mind was in a blur. What do I keep? What do I get rid of?

Paul did a great job packing and they blessed me abundantly. Then I awoke at 3:00 a.m. to write an inventory list, put things back in order, and gather supplies for a very poor lady with seven children. Her husband was murdered last year. When He was driving a truck, he was robbed and stabbed. They are in desperate need of clothing and other supplies.

I believed God was speaking to me, preparing me for a change. My devotions were very meaningful that morning. I read Oswald Chambers, My Utmost for His Highest. That day's date said: "*Never object to the intense sensitivity of the Spirit of God in you when he is instructing you down to the last detail.*"

I also read in Ezekiel 12:3 *"Therefore, son of man, prepare your belongings for captivity, and go into captivity by day in their sight."* I believed God was calling me to get ready – to prepare my belongings – for He was coming to take us away. I believed we would leave Madagascar sooner than we thought a month ago. The Lord had told me to get ready. Be prepared.

The testing of one's faith produces self-control and brings about pure gold as from a refiner's fire. My faith had not been tested like this since the time I sensed God spoke to me to marry Todd.

Everybody sees with different eyes. Todd was still not too sure about my thinking that the Lord was going to have us leave Madagascar sooner than we thought. Once again, we did not agree.

I wrote the following in my journal:

Friday, Oct. 12th.
Oswald Chambers talks on today's date about Moses – who heard the call of God, but then went through a process of 40 years of discipline and training. "Moses had realized that he was the one to deliver the people, but he had to be trained and disciplined by God first. He was right in his individual perspective, but he was not the person for the work until he had learned true fellowship and oneness with God."

Perhaps this is what God is doing with me. I have heard His call. Now it is His period of testing, enduring, waiting with patience and grace. Lord, cause me to be faithful - to listen to your voice, heed your call and be faithful with the little things. I love you, Lord Jesus. Amen

Tuesday, Oct 8th
Today I took our trunks to be shipped back to the USA. They will be sent in a portion of a container with another missionary family

who is leaving Madagascar to work in another post. If a prophecy is true, it will be brought about. There is no forcing it before its time, or it will be miscarried...aborted...or not fully developed. As a pregnant mother anxiously awaits the birth of her child, a servant of God awaits the will of their Father...yet the timing is unknown.

We were wardens for the American Community in Madagascar. At the end of October, we received the following document.

The FBI administration had concluded on October 29, 2001 that based on information developed, there may be additional terrorist attacks within the United States and against the United States interests over the next week. The administration views this information as credible, but unfortunately, it does not contain specific information as to the type of attack or specific targets.

Consequently, a terrorist threat advisory update has been issued to 18,000 law enforcement agencies across the country through the National Law enforcement telecommunications system known as NLETS. We have notified Law Enforcement to continue on highest alert and to notify immediately the FBI of any unusual or suspicious activity.

We have no indication that the U.S. Embassy in Antananarivo is under any particular threat from international terrorism. As recent events have shown, however, safety from terrorism can no longer be taken for granted.

V
Christmas

Christmas traditions were still enjoyed in the McGregor household. Even though I had to pull the Christmas stockings out of the suitcase, I was thankful to still be in Madagascar at Christmas time. As with every year, we made a lovely Christmas candy village with local biscuits and various types of candy. Todd made the village church, myself the school, Corbi and Charese each a house and Lindy, a teenage friend who was living with us, decorated the park. Placed neatly in the fireplace (it was summer time in the Southern hemisphere), it was a lovely sight as it lit up with tea candles on Christmas Eve!

A manger to one side of the fireplace, with the wise men and shepherds still *"walking"* to baby Jesus. In the midst of the evergreen branches laid the brown hand-carved Malagasy sculpture. Dania, our house-help, had been preparing food for the past week. Quiche, pizza, sweets, cookies, treats. We prepared for an open house for 100 guests after the Christmas Eve service, another McGregor tradition.

I really thought God spoke to me about an evacuation. I was prepared. My bags were still packed upstairs. But here we were on Christmas... *Silent Night, Holy Night, All is calm, all is bright.*

My faith began to waiver. *Was it just my way of* "coping" *or did I really think that God might have spoken? Was I silly or wrong in thinking so? What does it really matter if I am* "wrong" *anyway, doesn't God look at the heart, instead? What lessons have I learned through this experience? What has God taught me?*

Faith is like a car with wheels on. If I had sat complacent in Christ when He really did speak to me, then I would have not been acting out my faith.

In my many years in Madagascar, I have seen scores of broken down vehicles (including ours, unfortunately!) One of the most hilarious sights is to see the body of a car on top of a wooden cart pushed by several men.

Faith is just not the metal shell of a car excluding wheels! Faith has wheels on! Faith is putting into action what we believe we have heard from God.

On the last day of the year 2001, I wrote in my journal Presiding Bishop Frank T. Griswold's description of prayer. *"Prayer sensitizes us and makes us able to listen and pick up subtleties or things we might otherwise miss."*

The New Year's Day of 2002 arrived and I refused to unpack my suitcases.

VI
Waiting on God Develops Intimacy

Why does the Father make us wait sometimes for long periods of time for the answer? Waiting on God develops intimacy.

I really put my faith on the line. I told many friends about the dream I had in August. In faith, I packed my suitcase in September, shipped mementos back to the USA, and told others my dream. In October, I was bold, but in January I was stagnant.

Presidential elections were on December 16th. Although there were still some tense moments, we were still living in Madagascar. It did not look like the fulfillment of that dream was going to come about. Would that label me as a *"false prophet?"* or *"a misinterpreter of dreams?"*

On January 18th and 19th, I documented in my journal. Habakkuk 2:23 *"Write the vision and make it plain on tablets, that he may run who reads it. For the vision is yet for an appointed time; but at the end it will speak, and it will not lie. Though it tarries; wait for it; because it will surely come, it will not tarry."*

The Lord was quickening my heart again, calling me to be ready. I still believed the time was near. The Lord was revealing new aspects of my dream. Puzzle pieces I did not understand previously now fit together, one by one.

The girls and I talked often about the possibility of leaving. I asked them if they were ready. They believed they were. God had been preparing them to leave Madagascar even though they knew no other home.

Do not be afraid, mom, Corbi told me one day when my faith was wavering. *Dad thinks I am crazy.* I said back to her.

She chuckled and suggested: *Do not listen to him.*

VII
Political Turmoil

In February, things began to get hot.

We wrote an email to friend and supporters, urging them to pray for us and the country.

Dear Friends,
This is another update on the political situation here in Madagascar. Please use it not only as information, but also to keep this country in your prayers.

After a week of intense meetings, mediated by the president of the African Organization for Unity, the representatives of the opposition leader, and the representatives of the president broke off negotiations today. Just two hours ago the opposition leader, Marc Ravalomanana, announced that he would take over power unilaterally as president of Madagascar. He still claims that he won the December 16th election outright by a majority vote.

Last night there was an attempted assassination of the opposition leader, and he has urged the protesters to surround his house and the mayor's palace, because the military has called back all his personal security guards. We have finished the fourth week of the second round of strikes, and these have virtually brought the country to a standstill. The post office and government offices have been closed for the last month. Banks and the airport have been open sporadically. We have had a fuel shortage in the last week due to government (it is alleged) blocking crude coming from the coast where the refinery is located. It is estimated that the textile and clothing companies (Gap, Eddie Bauer) are loosing between 12-14 million dollars a day.

The American School, where Patsy is working, and which Corbi is attending (the opposition leader's son goes to the same school), has been re-opened, and life is somewhat "normal". The missionary school, which Charese attends, is also in session. However, it is on the other side of town and may need to become a boarding school if fuel continues to be in shortage. Our lives continue to go on ... we avoid the peaceful demonstrations held downtown and have stored up a bit of fuel (we learned from the strikes in 1991)...but we do wonder what will happen next. President Ratsiraka had stated previously that he would not use force unless the opposition leader took power. It is amazing to note that for the past four weeks all demonstrations by the opposition leader have been peaceful. But we are all very concerned about how Ratsiraka will handle the opposition's unilateral move to take power. We fear it may be by force and are reminded of the words the Archbishop said three weeks ago, "There will be bloodshed for sure."

Thank you for keeping our family, this country and the Malagasy people in your prayers.

Todd and Patsy McGregor

Emails from friends were an encouragement to us at such a desperate time.

Dear Patsy and Todd:
   Thank you for your update on the situation at present. It brings back memories of my missionary days and the uncertainty that it imposes on your life and the life of those you love around you.

   The only sure thing that we have is to pray and to trust that God will continue protecting all of you and the church. During the hard times like these it is difficult to "really" believe those words that sound like empty promises. After being away now for over a year from the foreign mission field I can tell you that God was always there protecting and caring for us, our families and friends.

   I also know that now is the time when those that you have been ministering to are looking at your faithfulness and trust in God. At the same time they know that it is their struggle for freedom and democracy. You can only support them morally and with your prayers.

   I apologize for trying to be an old missionary guru but I feel that our Lord is moving me to share these words of assurance and power. I remember what Archbishop Tutu used to share with me in our email conversations when things were going quite bad in Honduras: "When things are going marvelous and everything is working right, there is no question that God is in control. But when things are a mess and nothing seems to go right then we know that there is no question that God is in control." *Our God is caring with us in the good and the bad times. It seems that things are not very hot at the time but be assured that you are not alone. God is there and we are here. Let me know as things develop.*

*Love and prayers from your friends in Miami. I am proud that
I can say that I am your bishop.*
  Blessings,
  +Leo

The political situation was growing tenser by the day. Schools
were closed, "*Dead days*" declared. Nothing was open. The airport,
public transportation, fuel stations, schools, banks, shops - everything
was closed.

The incumbent President threatened to cut off the electricity in
the capital if demonstrations continued. There was talk of sabotaging
the lake that supplied all the water for the capital. The roads, leading
to all port cities, were blocked. There was threat of civil war. We
had a friend who was the head of distributing the fuel for the entire
country. He said that there was only enough automobile fuel to last
until the weekend and only enough electrical fuel for another week.
Unless something was done, the capital would come to a standstill.
Everything became deathly quiet. No cars were on the streets, no
people walked to work. Even the dogs seemed to be on strike as they
had stopped barking!

My heart was very heavy for the country of Madagascar. I
prayed when I read the paper. I prayed when I drove on the roads. I
prayed when I saw my Malagasy friends suffer for the sake of
righteousness. They were fighting for a cause and I supported them
in prayer. *O Lord, give them wisdom.*

On February 22nd, a state of national emergency was declared
across the entire territory for a period of three months. On March 1st
martial law was imposed.

Finally, Todd was ceding to the idea that we may need to leave
Madagascar earlier than expected.

VIII
Evacuation

Packing only their most valuable possessions, people were leaving the country overnight. At the end of the school day on Friday, friends would say, "H*ave a nice weekend*". Monday students were absent. We were told they left the country. The American Embassy called a mandatory evacuation for all "*non-essential government personnel.*"

Companies demanded that employees leave the country. Charese's missionary school became a boarding school, as there was no gas to travel from one side of the city to another. Like an unwanted scene in a video movie, the American School year was "*fast-forwarded*". Nine weeks of school were condensed into four. The school year was over in early May.

My dream became reality. We left Madagascar earlier than anticipated.

IX
Goodbyes Are Never Easy

> *There is a time for everything,*
> *and a season for every activity under heaven:*
> *A time to be born, And a time to die...*
> *A time to plant and a time to uproot...*
> *A time to tear down and a time to build...*
> *A time to weep and a time to laugh...*
> (Ecclesiastes 3:2-4)

It was the first time I had seen Archbishop Rémi cry. We had been together at weddings, funerals, and ordinations, but in my eleven years in Madagascar, I had never seen him cry. On 14 May 2002, tears slid down his cheeks.

Not one was with dry eyes that day. As true to Malagasy custom, several people had come to the airport to say goodbye. Just as the day we arrived, our loyal Malagasy friends were always present.

The day before, at the dedication of the lay-training center, Todd spoke to a gathering of a few hundred, *What makes it so difficult to say goodbye is not what we have done, but the friendships that have been nurtured, the relationships that have been built.*

With our Malagasy colleagues and friends, we had traveled into the rain forest, spent time in fellowship, performed weddings, wept through funerals, celebrated anniversaries, endured graduations, visited the sick, attended confirmations and baptisms, shared meals and broken bread together at the Lord's Table. This country had been our home, and we had shared our lives together with our friends here.

Mandrampihaona, or "until later" were the words we exchanged in those final minutes, stressing the fact that someday, somewhere, we would see each other again.

Bags were packed, presents received, tickets and passports in hand. It was time to go. Either coming, or going, God's will is not always easy.

We exchanged a strong embrace. I gave Archbishop Rémi my final hug, and said, *Thank you for the best eleven years of my life.* The Archbishop, comfortable with preaching before thousands, shared my embrace and began to cry.

Bibliography

Brandt, Hilary. *Guide to Madagascar.* United States/United
    Kingdom: Brandt Publications/Globe Requot Press, 1994.
Heale, Jay. *Cultures of the World.* New York/London/Sydney: Times
    Editions Pte Ltd, 1998.
Murphy, Delva. *Muddling Through in Madagascar.* New York:
    Overlook Press, New York, 1989.
Oswald Chambers. *My Utmost for His Highest.* Grand Rapids,
    Michigan: Discovery Hose Publishers, 1963.
Oluonye, Mary N. *Madagascar.* Minneapolis: Carol Rhoda Books,
    Inc., 2000.
Swaney, Deanna and Robert Willcox. *Madagascar & Comoros.*
    Australia: Lonely Planet, 1994.